Time Out Coach!

Offense Plays & Last Second Situations

Written by:

Coach João da Costa

AuthorHouse™ LLC
1663 Liberty Drive
Bloomington, IN 47403
www.authorhouse.com
Phone: 1-800-839-8640

Published by AuthorHouse 02/20/2014

ISBN: 978-1-4918-6157-8 (sc)
ISBN: 978-1-4918-6158-5 (e)

Library of Congress Control Number: 2014902209

Any people depicted in stock imagery provided by Thinkstock are models,
and such images are being used for illustrative purposes only.
Certain stock imagery © Thinkstock.

This book is printed on acid-free paper.

Because of the dynamic nature of the Internet, any web addresses or links contained in this book may have changed
since publication and may no longer be valid. The views expressed in this work are solely those of the author and do
not necessarily reflect the views of the publisher, and the publisher hereby disclaims any responsibility for them.

Time Out Coach!

Offense Plays & Last Second Situations

Written by:

Coach João da Costa

Dedicated to boys:
Tyler and Russell

Key

[C] [1]	Coach 1
○ •	Player with the Ball
®	Rebounding Player
① ② ③ ④ ⑤	Offensive Players
❶ ❷ ❸ ❹ ❺	Defensive Players
——————▶	Cut
------------▶	Pass
∿∿∿——▶	Dribble
———————┤	Screen

Table of Contents

Introduction

This book was written to provide coaches some tools to be successful securing the win during those last moments of a tight game. It is a play book that will provide last seconds basketball plays, tactics and strategies to help you win the close game. It is my intention that coaches at any level can utilize this book and select plays which fit their particular style and program.

Each play can be adapted to provide scoring opportunities for the best players on any team. Remember; what works for one team may not work for another so it is important to consider your specific player's talent and abilities as you select plays from this book. While these plays are designed to get a specific player a shot at the basket, most good plays offer options, so for example, if the play is designed to provide an option for the shooting guard, you should provide a secondary option for another player in case the initial action is stopped.

Preparation is the key to success. Practice and rehearsal for special situations will ensure your team is confident to react and execute when they have a special possession situation. While it is easy to put aside time for offense or defense, Coaches should schedule time every practice to go over last second situations. Evaluate and select those plays that your team can execute and make their own. Make sure to cover the plays individually and then scrimmage to practice the execution. Frequent execution and discussion of the techniques will prepare the team for those moments during the game and they can confidently take advantage of the situation.

As you read this book, keep in mind it's better to just have a few good plays that your players become really good at rather than overloading your team with too many options.

Good luck, to you Coach! I hope these plays are helpful for your basketball program.

Early Offense
"Quick Set" Plays

Many professional teams run an "early offense" or "quick" set. This occurs when a player advances the ball up the court quickly after a field goal or made free throw.

Most early offense plays depend on a quick inbounds and pass advance to reach the offensive operating area before the defenders can set up in the front court.

If a team has good big players, the early offense should give those players the opportunity to post up and score. "Bigs" should run rim to rim with the trailing big looking to hit the other big on the run or on early post up. **GET THE BALL INTO THE POST.**

If the shooting guards are the strength of the team, then they can run off screens for the shots. Whatever the team chooses to do, should be based on a system that gets your good players early shots and then flows into the offense that team is running at the time.

This type of constant attacks does not give the defense time to re-group and may catch them out of position for a quality shot early in the possession.

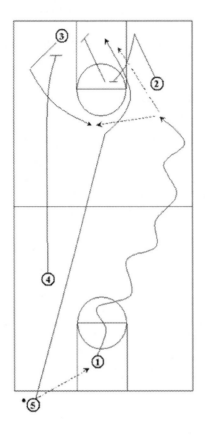

Elbow

Player 5 inbounds the ball to 1.

Player 1 pushes the ball quickly up right side to the wing.

Player 2 cuts toward the basket, stops, then moves up the lane to set a back screen for 5.

Player 1 looks to pass to 5 after he cuts off the back screen to the basket.

If the pass to the post is denied, then players 2 and 4 down screen for 3.

Player 3 comes off the double screen to get the ball from 1 at top of the key for a jump shot.

Note: Players 4 and 5 are interchangeable.

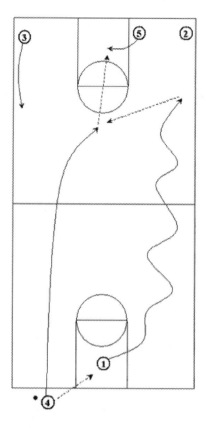

Spread Wide

Player 4 inbounds the ball to 1.
Player 1 advances the ball up the court and reverses to 4 at top the key.
Player 5 seals his defender in the lane to get the high low pass from 4 for a shot under the basket.
Players 2 and 3 stay wide to eliminate help defense.

Note: This is a simple quick set where you can get an easy basket from the Big Man. If player 5 cannot get the ball then just go right into your half-court offense.

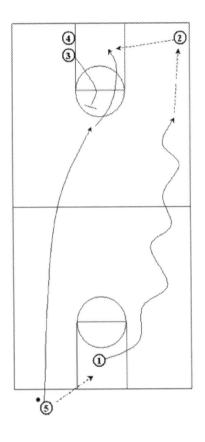

Stack Three

Here is another simple early offense or quick set that gives you a different look for your Big Man to score.

Player 5 inbounds the ball to 1.

Player 1 dribbles up the court looking to pass to 2 at corner.

Player 3 back screens 5's defender.

Player 5 cuts to the basket to receive a pass from 2 for lay-up.

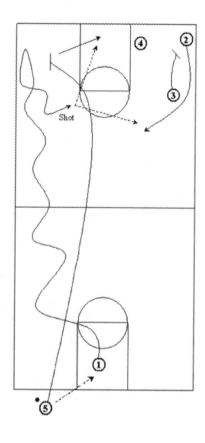

Turn and Go "TG"

Player 5 inbounds the ball to 1.
Player 1 pushes the ball quickly up the left side.
Player 5, the trailer, ball screens for 1 at the left wing.
Player 1 runs a screen and roll with 5.
At the same time 3 down screens for 2 at corner.
Player 1 can look for 2 at wing for shot.

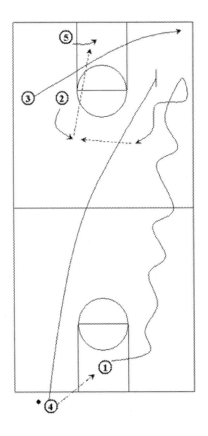

Two Up

Player 4 inbounds the ball to 1.
Player 1 pushes the ball up the court to the right wing.
Player 4, the trailer, ball screens for 1.
Player 3, clears out to opposite corner.
Player 2, pops out to get the ball from 1 and quickly executes a high low pass to 5 inside the lane for a shot.

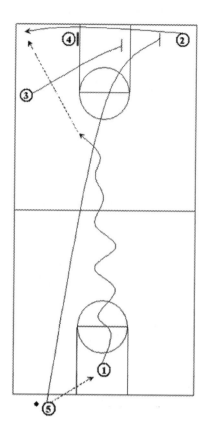

Baseline Shot " BS"

Player 5 inbounds the ball to 1.

Player 1 dribbles up the court.

Player 2 cuts baseline by receiving a staggered screens from 5, 3 and 4.

Player 1 hits 2 at the corner for turnaround jump shot.

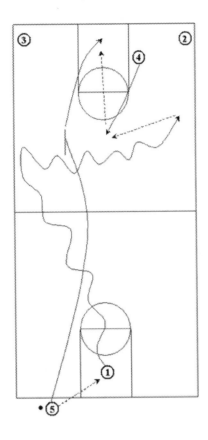

Quick Drag

Player 5 inbounds the ball to 1.

Player 1 drives off a late "drag" screen and roll set by 5.

As the screen and roll takes place 4 flashes high to get the ball from 1.

Player 4 looks to hit 5 in the lane for a shot under the basket.

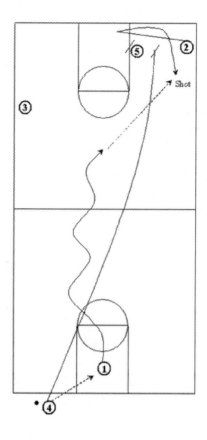

Fake Two

Player 4 inbounds the ball to 1.

Player 1 pushes the ball up the court looking for 2.

Player 2 fakes into the lane then comes off the screens set by 5 and 4, to receive ball from 1 at wing for a jump shot.

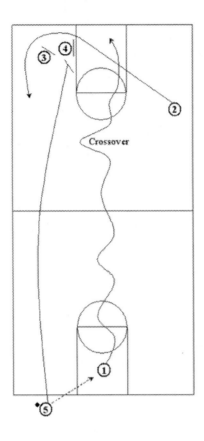

345 Down

Player 5 inbounds the ball to 1.

Player 1 advances the ball up the court.

As 1 crosses half court, 2 cuts through the lane to receive screens set by 5, 4, and 3.

Player 1 looks to pass to 2 at wing for a shot or he drives all the way to the basket for lay-up.

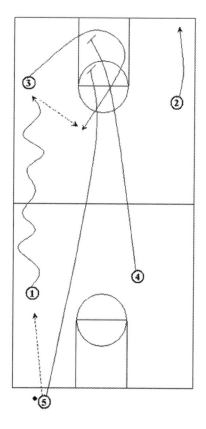

Three Loop

Player 5 inbounds the ball to 1.

Player 1 advances the ball quickly up the left side.

Player 2 slides down to the corner as 3 flashes to the top off staggered screens set by 4 and 5.

Player 1 hits 3 at the top of the key for a shot.

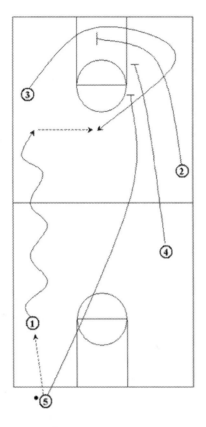

Three Together

Player 5 inbounds the ball to 1.
Player 1 advances the ball quickly up the left side.
As 1 crosses half court, 3 cuts through the lane to staggered screens set
by 2, 4 and 5.
Player 1 hits 3 at three point arch for a shot.

Note: Players 4 and 5 are interchangeable

Full Court Transition Drills

Use these drills to work on your transition offense. Players can run up and down the court to improve their passing and shooting skills.

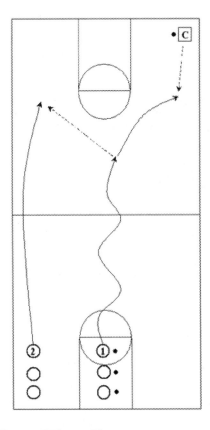

Full Court Wings Shots

Place a coach at right corner with the ball.
Player 1 pushes the ball up the court and passes to 2 for a jump shot at left wing then cuts to the right wing to receive the ball from the coach for a shot.

Note: Player 2 gets his own rebound and feeds the coach.

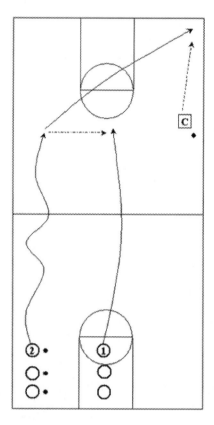

Middle to Corner Shooting Drills
This time place a coach at wing with the ball.

Player 2 pushes the ball quickly up the left side and passes to 1 at top of the key for a jump shot then cuts through the lane to the right deep corner to receive the ball from the coach for a turn-around jump shot.

Note: Player 1 gets his own rebound and feeds the coach.

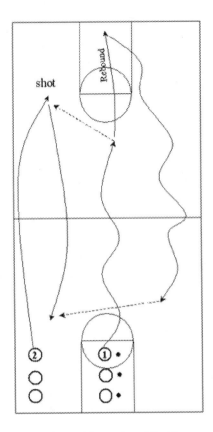

Hit Me at Wing Shooting Drills

Player 1 pushes the ball quickly up the court and hits 2 at wing.
Player 1 takes the ball out of the net and dribbles down the court looking
for 2 for a second shot.

Note: Make sure the players score twice in a row.

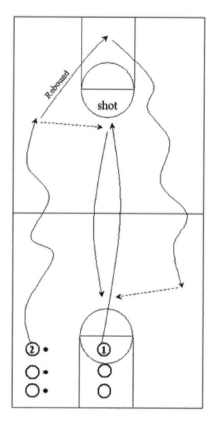

Hit Me at Middle Shooting Drills

Player 2 pushes the ball quickly up the left side and passes to 1 at top of key for a jump shot.
Player 2 takes the ball out of the net and dribbles down the court looking for 1 for another jump shot.

Note: Make sure the players score twice in a row.

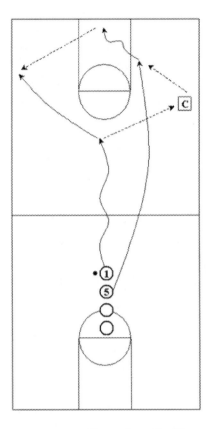

Trailer Lay-up & Shooting Drills

Player 1 pushes the ball up the court and passes to the coach at wing.
Player 5, the trailer, cuts to the basket to receive the pass from the coach
for lay-up.
Player 5 quickly takes the ball out of the net and hits 1 at wing for a shot.

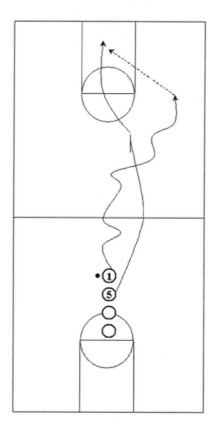

Pick & Roll Lay-up & Shooting Drill

Player 1 pushes the ball up the court and 5 sets a pick at top of key. Player 5 rolls to the basket to get the pass from 1 for a lay-up.

Note: On the second attempt, run the same drill, this time 1 takes a shot at the wing and 5 goes for the rebound.

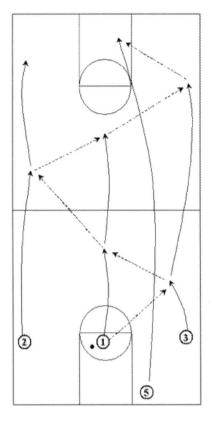

Three Man with Trailer Lay-up Drill

Start the drill with the trailer, 5 the big man, behind the ball.

The point guard will push the ball up the court with 2 and 3 passing back and forth.

Whoever has the ball at the wing looks to feed 5 who cuts into the lane for the lay-up.

On the way back, player 1 takes the ball out of the net and runs the same drill back down the court looking for the trailer(5) to finish the drill with lay-up.

Post-Up Plays

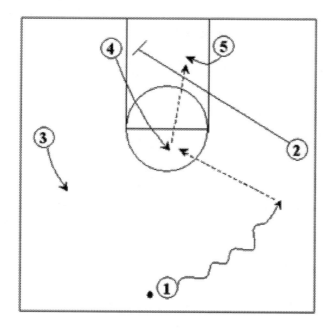

Up Four

Player 1 dribbles to the right wing.

Player 2 screens against 4's defender at low block.

Player 4 flashes to the free throw line to receive the pass from 1.

Player 4 can either take the shot or pass high low to 5 inside the lane.

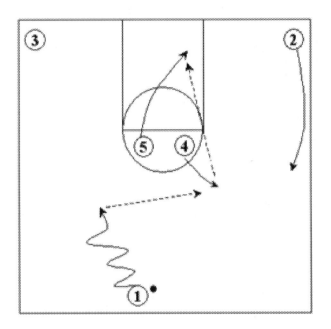

54 Down

Player 4 pops out to get the pass from 1 at top of key.

Player 2 comes up to the wing.

Player 5 cuts diagonally across the lane to the right block and seals his defender to receive high low pass from 4 for a shot under the basket.

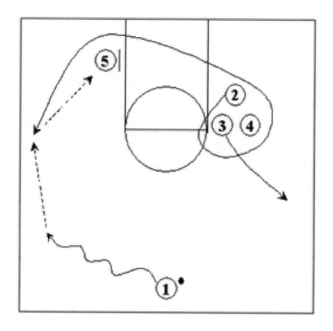

Loop Around 34

Player 2 begins the play by looping around 3 and 4 at right wing area, then crosses the lane to receive a screen from 5 at left low post block. Player 2 comes off the screen to get the ball from 1 at left wing. Player 2 can shoot or feed 5 in the low post position for one-on-one to the hoop.

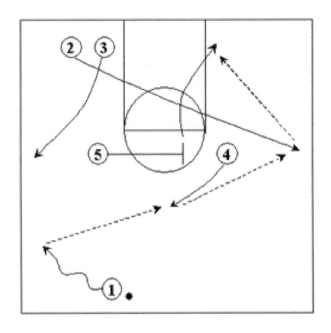

23 Pick Four

The play starts when players 2 and 3 flash to the wings.
Player 5 screens for 4 then rolls to basket.
Player 1 hits 4 at top of key and 4 quickly passes to 2 at wing.
Player 2 executes a entry pass to 5 at low post block.

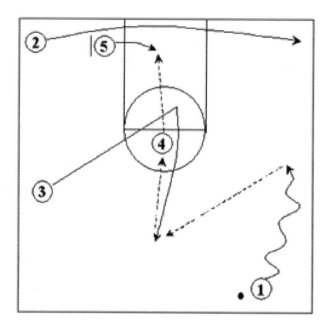

Curl Up

Player 2 clears out by cutting opposite corner.

Player 3 curls around 4 to top of key to receive the ball from 1.

Player 3 catches the ball and quickly passes to 4.

Player 4 looks to feed 5 inside the lane for a shot under the basket.

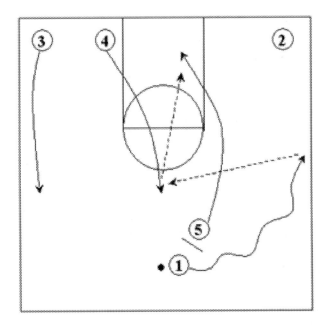

Flash Four

Player 4 flashes to the top of key.

Player 5 ball screens for 1 then rolls to basket.

Player 1 passes to 4 and 4 looks to pass to 5 inside the box.

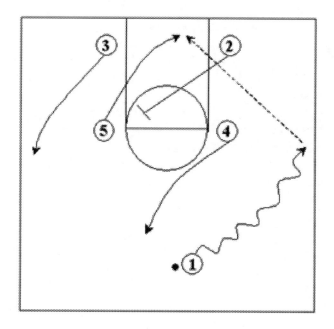

Box Five

Player 1 dribbles to the right wing.

Player 4 pops out to the top of key.

Player 3 comes up to the left wing.

Player 2 back screens 5's defender at high post.

Player 5 cuts behind the screen to the ball side block to get the ball from 1 for a shot under the basket.

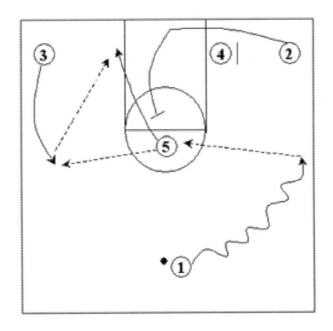

42 Pick

Player 1 dribbles to the right wing to hit 5 at free throw line.

Player 3 flashes to the left wing to receive the ball from 5.

Player 4 baseline screen for 2 then 2 comes off the screen to back screen 5's defender.

Player 5 cuts to the ball side block to receive a reverse pass from 3 for one-on-one to the basket.

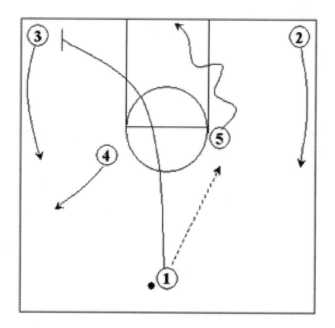

All the Way

Player 4 pops out to the left wing.

Player 1 passes to 5 at elbow and down screens for 3 at corner.

Player 2 comes up to the ball side wing.

Player 5 dribbles all do way to basket.

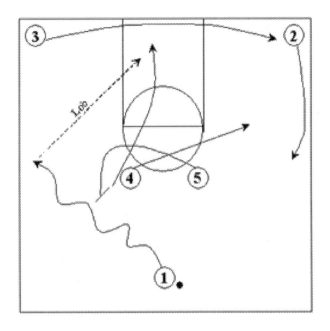

Big Switch

Player 2 comes up to the wing.

Player 3 clears out to opposite corner.

Players 4 and 5 switch positions at top of the nail.

Player 5 ball screens for 1 then rolls to the basket.

Player 1 quickly makes an over the top lob pass to 5 for a lay-up.

Quick Shot Plays

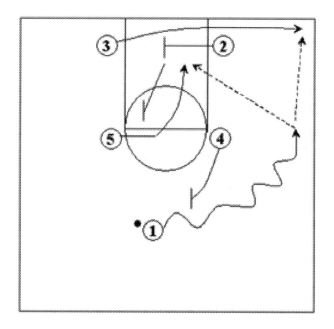

Two Run

Player 4 sets a ball screen for 1.

Player 1 dribbles to the right wing.

Player 2 cross screen for 3 then back screens 5's defender at elbow.

Player 1 looks to pass to 5 inside the lane or 3 at deep corner for a shot.

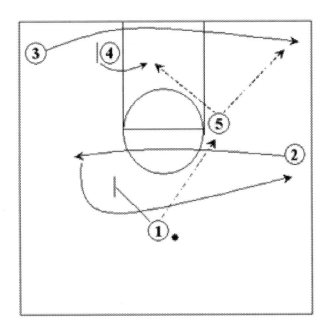

Side-To-Side

Player 2 begins with a cut to opposite wing

Player 1 passes to 5 at high post while 4 sets a baseline screen for 3, who cuts to the right corner.

Player 5 looks to pass to 3 at the corner or 4 who seals his player inside the lane.

If player 5 cannot pass to either 3 or 4, then 1 screens for 2.

Player 2 cuts to ball side wing to receive a pass from 5 for a shot.

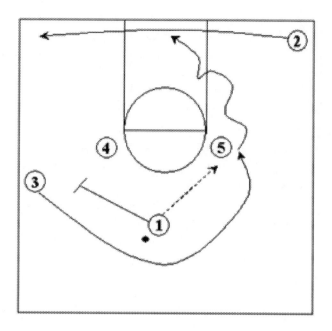

Go Three

Player 2 clears out to opposite corner.

Player 1 passes to 5 at high post then screens for 3 at wing.

Player 3 cuts toward 5 to get a hand off then drives to the basket for lay-up or steps back for a shot.

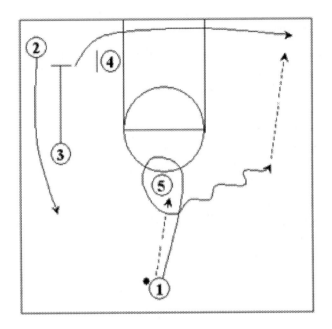

Loop Five

Player 1 passes to 5 and loops around him for a hand off at top of key.
Player 3 down screens for 2 and receives a screen from 4 making his way
to ball side corner.
Player 1 hits 3 for a shot.

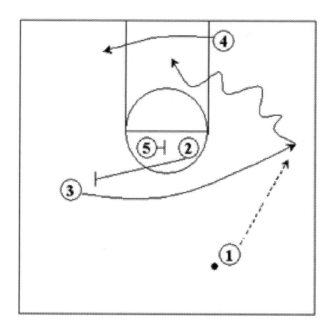

52 Side

Player 4 crossing to opposite block.
Player 5 screens for 2 and 2 screens for 3 at left wing.
Player 3 cuts to ball side wing to receive a pass from 1.
Player 3 drives to the hoop for one-on-one situation.

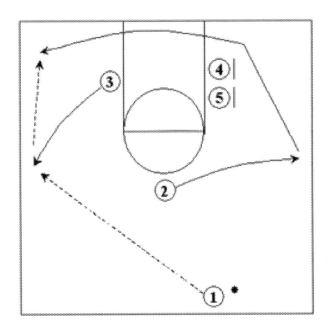

Baseline Two

Player 2 breaks to the right wing.
Player 3 pops out to the left wing to receive the ball from 1.
Players 4 and 5 set a double screen for 2, who cuts to opposite corner,
looking for the pass from 3 for a shot.

Note: If player 2 cannot shoot then 5 cuts into the lane to get the entry
pass from 2 on the ball side block.

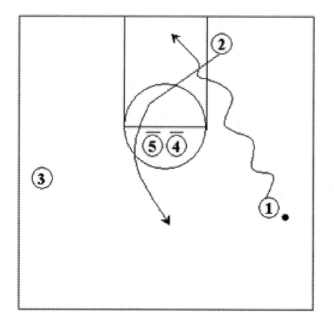

54 Lay-Up

Players 4 and 5 double screen for 2 at free throw line.
While player 2 flashes to the top of the key, pretending to get the ball,
player 1 attacks the basket for lay-up.

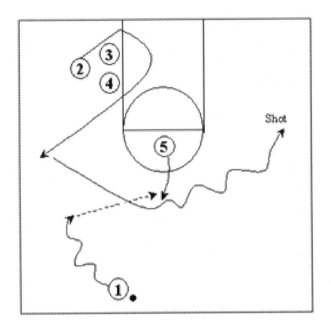

Triangle Baseline

Player 1 hits 5 at the top of the key.
Player 2 cuts through the lane and pops out to the left wing then sprints toward 5 to receive hand off for a pull up jump shot at the right wing.

Note: If player 2 cannot shoot then 5 will cut to the ball side block looking for the ball for one-on-one to the basket.

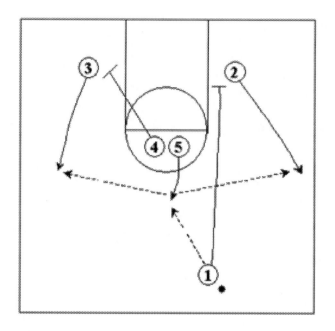

45 High Post

Player 5 steps high to receive the ball from 1.

Player 1, after passing to 5, down screens for 2, at the same time 4 down screens for 3.

Player 5 looks to pass to either 2 or 3 at wings for a quick shot.

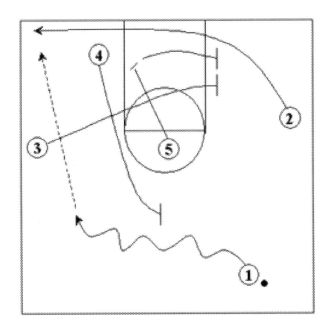

Two Corners

Player 5 begins by down screen for 4 then moves to the right block.
Player 4 flashes to the top of key to ball screen for 1.
Player 3 cuts through the lane to the mid post to double screen with 5 against 2's defender.
Player 1 dribbles to the left wing looking to pass to 2 at deep corner for a turn-around jump shot.

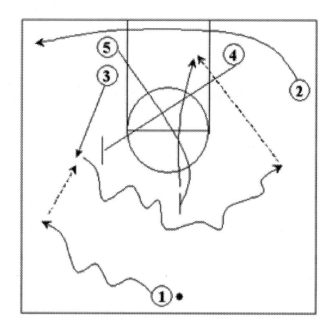

53 Pick & Roll

Player 2 clears out by cutting opposite corner.

Player 3 pops out to the left wing to receive the ball from 1.

At the same time players 4 and 5 flash to the top of key to ball screen for 3.

Player 3 dribbles to the right wing looking for 5 who rolls to the basket for a shot.

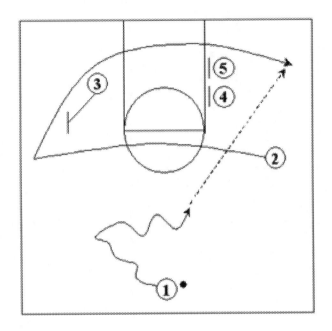

Wild Shot

Player 2 begins by breaking to opposite wing, at the same time 3 pops out to set a screen against 2's defender.

Player 2 continues and cuts opposite corner to receive a double screen set by 4 and 5.

Player 1 hits 2 for a turn-around jump shot at deep corner.

Full Court
Man-to-Man
Press Breakers

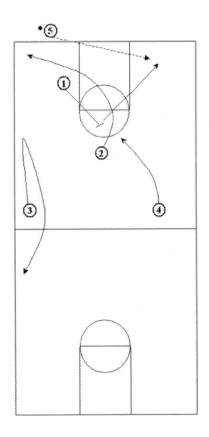

Falcon

First Option

Player 5 is the inbounder.

Player 1 back screens for 2 then rolls to the weak side short corner asking for ball.

Player 2 cuts toward inbounder 5.

Player 4 moves to top of key looking for the pass incase 1 or 2 don't get the ball.

Player 3 breaks towards the baseline reverse pivot and sprints down the court.

Player 5 looks to inbound the ball to 1 or 2.

Note: The primary objective of breaking a full-court press is to get the ball in-bounds.

Have one of your post players inbound the ball as quickly as possible after a made basket, before the defense gets set. Have the same player take it out each time and make sure he knows that is his assignment. Don't take the ball out directly under the basket. The backboard will become another defensive player if you look to make a high, long pass.

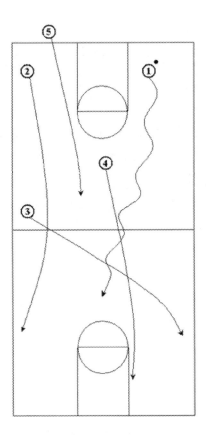

Falcon

Start the Break.
Player 1 takes the ball down the court.
Player 2 fills the right lane and 3 the left lane.
Player 4 gets on the low post position opposite to 5 the "trailer".

Note: Spread your offense as much as possible to make the defense cover a great deal of the court.

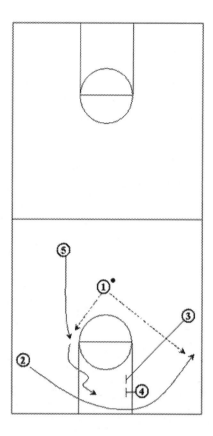

Falcon

Quick Shot
Player 1 looks for 2 who is cutting to opposite wing by receiving a double set screen by 3 and 4 at the mid-post.
At the same time 5 cuts into the lane for a possible pass for lay-up.

Note: Once you cross half-court, attack, attack, attack. The press is broken. Attack the basket and get some easy points. Press is vulnerable to lay-ups and short jump shots. Be patient; try to work the ball to an open player.

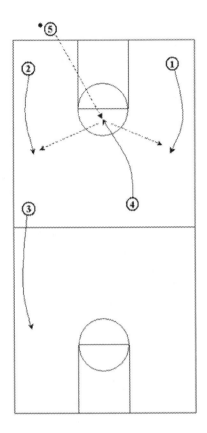

Falcon

Second Option

Suppose the defense is denying the pass to players 1 and 2 then player 4
will get the inbound pass inside the box.

Player 4 looks to pass either 2 or 1 to push the ball down the court.

Player 3 sprints release down the court.

Note: Make sure your receivers come to the ball! They should attack
each reception with the same intensity that the defense does. This cannot
be overemphasized. Have them come and meet the ball before they stop.
Then catch with two hands, hop stop, and establish a pivot foot. This
gives them much more latitude to attack the defense. Once the ball is
inbounded, look up the sideline for an open man.

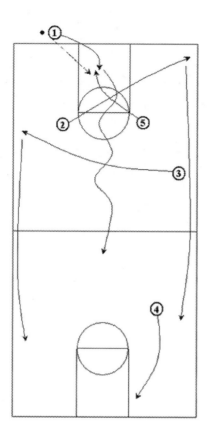

Big Men Ball

Here is a simple play against press.

Player 3 begins the play by breaking to the ball side wing.

Player 2 cuts opposite side to the deep corner.

Player 5 cuts through the lane to receive the inbound pass from 1.

Player 5 catches the ball and quickly hands off to 1.

Players 2 and 3 run the outlet.

Player 5 is the trailer.

Player 4 stays at low post position.

Note: Don't be intimidated or fearful. Attack the pressure with the objective of scoring.

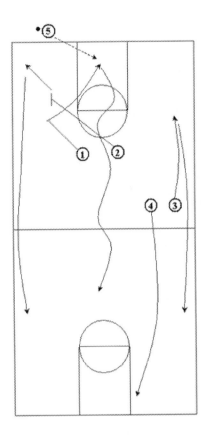

Twelve

First option

Player 4 sprints release down the court.

Player 3 moves up to be an option to catch the inbound pass from 5.

Player 1 breaks toward the ball side wing asking for ball.

Player 2 follows him and back screens 1's defender then opens up to the ball side corner looking for a possible pass from 5.

Player 1 comes off the screen to receive the inbound pass.

Player 1 pushes the ball down the court for a quick break.

Note: Get the ball in quickly, before the defense can set up. Make sure you make a good inbound pass. Do not take the ball out from directly under your basket, or your passing lane may be restricted by the backboard

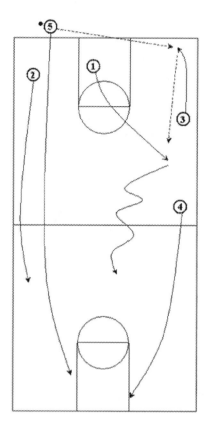

Twelve

Second Option

If player 5 cannot inbound pass to 1 then looks for 3 as second option at opposite corner.

Player 3 quickly looks for 1 to reverse the ball in the mid-court.

Player 1 takes the ball down the court.

Player 2 fills the right lane.

Player 3 fills the left lane.

Player 4 goes to the low post block.

Player 5 is the trailer.

Alternative: if the inbounder 5 decides to pass to 2, then 2 looks to pass to 1 at mid-court. If 2 cannot pass to 1 then 2 pushes the ball down the court. Player 1 fills the right lane and 3 fills the left lane.

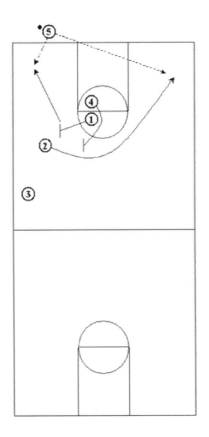

41 Side

First Option

Player 5 slaps the ball to start the movement of the team.

Players 4 and 1 set a staggered screen for 2.

Player 2 cuts to the weak side corner looking for the pass.

Player 1 after screens for 2 then rolls towards the baseline to get the inbound pass from 5.

Note: Most of the time the screener will be the one that will be open. The ball must be put in play as quickly as possible after the opponent scores.

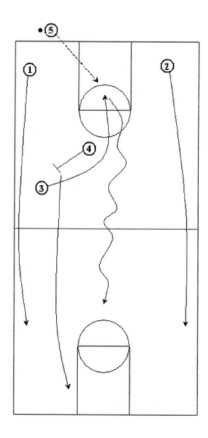

41 Side

Second Option

If player 5 cannot inbound the ball to 1 or 2 then player 4 back screens for 3 who cuts hard through the lane to get the ball from 5.
Player 3 advances the ball down the court starting the fast break while the wings run the outlet.

Note: Player 3 should look ahead and anticipate where he will pass the ball, even before he gets it. Once a press is broken, however, the defensive team is vulnerable to a potential fast break or open three-point opportunity since defensive players may be caught behind the play.

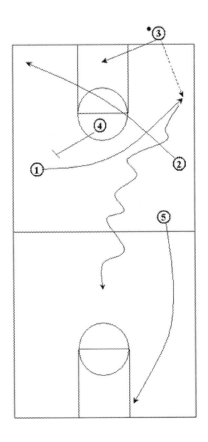

Atlanta

First Option

This is a great play against a team who pressure aggressively.

Inbound the ball quickly after a made basket.

Player 2 breaks to opposite corner.

Player 4 back screens for 1.

Player 1 comes off the screen, toward the ball, for a pass.

Player 3 inbounds the ball to 1 and steps in.

Keep player 3 back for a "safety" outlet pass from 1.

In this case 1 brings the ball down the court.

Player 5 cuts to the low post position.

Note: Instruct your team to set screens, freeing themselves from their men. On offense, there are four other players without the ball. Two screens should be set so that two offense players break free their man and are open to receive the ball.

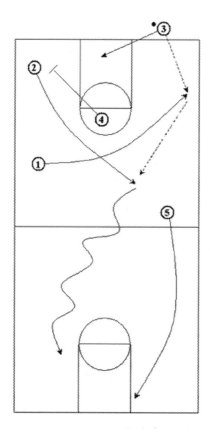

Atlanta

Second Option
If player 1 cannot advance the ball, then 4 screens for 2.
Player 2 cuts toward the middle to get the pass from 1.
Once player 2 gets the ball, he speed dribbles down the court, the press is beaten, and we are looking for lay-up.

Note: If player 1 cannot hit 2 at middle then he reverses the ball to 3.
Player 3 will push the ball down the right sideline.

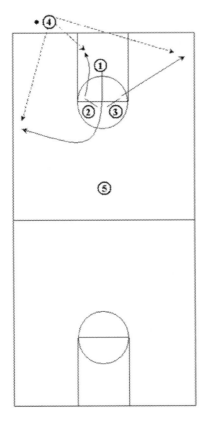

Diamond

First Option
Players 2 and 3 screen for 1, who cuts up between them to the ball side wing.
Player 3 breaks to opposite corner and 2 rolls to the baseline.
Player 4 has an option to inbound the ball to players 1, 2, and 3.

Note: Use V-cuts to get open and ball fakes to avoid telegraphing the pass. Be patient, be smart, and be confident.

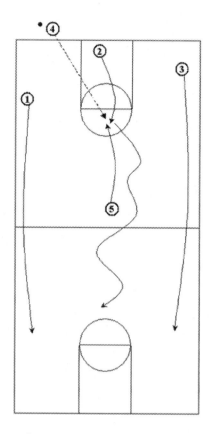

Diamond

Second Option

If player 4 cannot inbound the ball to 1, 2 or 3 then passes to 5 who hands off to 2.

Player 2 quickly pushes the ball down the court.

Players 1 and 3 run the lanes.

Player 5 will take the low post position.

Player 4 will be the trailer.

Note: One of my most important rules is to never pass back; always pass ahead. By passing back, a team has to beat the press twice because an opponent will set up a trap wherever players move to. Look up the court; don't look down at the ball when you dribble.

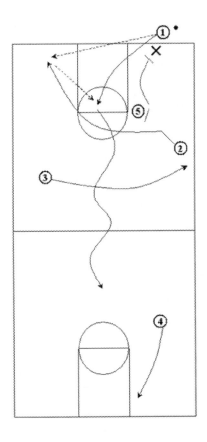

Arkansas

First option

This press breaker works extremely well against teams that pressure the inbound pass.

Player 5 begins by setting a screen for 2 who cuts to the opposite corner and 3 breaks to ball side wing.

Player 1 inbounds the ball to 2, while 5 screens 1's defender.

Player 1 should be wide open for the pass from 2, to start the break.

Note: Look for the open spots in the defense. Get open so your teammate can pass to you. Before you even get the ball, look to see where other open teammates are, so you will know where to pass to immediately. When you receive the ball, don't have your back turned. Immediately pivot and face down-court, so you can find an open teammate.

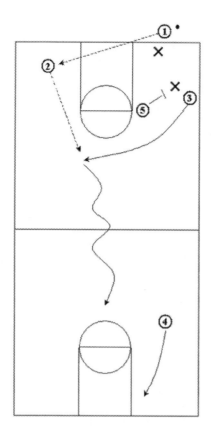

Arkansas

Second Option
When 2 receives the ball, this time 5 screens 3's defender.
Player 2 looks for 3 at mid-court, who will be wide open.
Player 3 advances the ball down the court to attack the basket.

Note: Whether you're in the baseline corner, or right before the half-court, or right beyond the half-court line, never pick your dribble up in a corner. You are a trap and turnover waiting to happen. Get the ball to the middle, if you give up your dribble it should only be to pass.

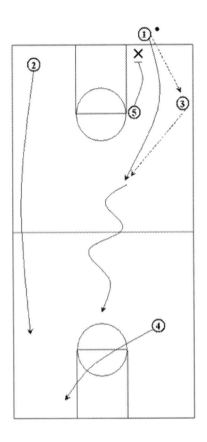

Arkansas

Third Option
If player 1 can't inbound pass to 2 then passes to 3 at ball side wing.
Player 5 back screens against 1's defender.
Player 1 cuts hard up the middle expecting the return pass from 3.
Player 1 can now attack, as the press is beaten.

Remember: Stay calm, see the floor, pass quickly, make sharp cuts, and "ATTACK!"

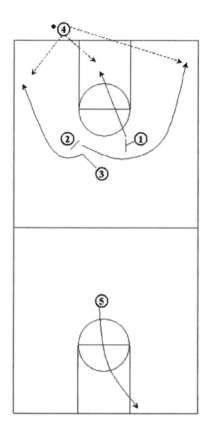

Triangle 231

This play requires everybody moving simultaneously setting good solid screens to get open.

Player 2 sets a pick for 3 and 3 comes off the screen to the ball side corner.

Player 1 screens for 2 then rolls into the lane looking for the pass, while 2 comes off the screen to the weak side corner.

Player 4, the inbounder, can pass to either 3, 1 or 2 to start the break.

Note: From an offensive perspective, it is essential to be prepared for full-court pressure. Players must be well drilled to make passes, pivots, cuts, and receptions without withering under a defensive onslaught. In addition, the offense must have a tactical plan for breaking the press, and the team must have absolute faith in that attack.

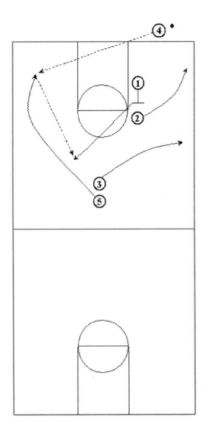

Get Together

Here is a good press break to confuse the defense team.
Players 3 and 5 break to the opposite sides, while 1 back screens for 2.
Player 4 inbound pass to 5, who then quickly passes to 1.
Player 1 should be wide open to start the break.

Note: This is a very effective play that can help to break the press easy and fast.

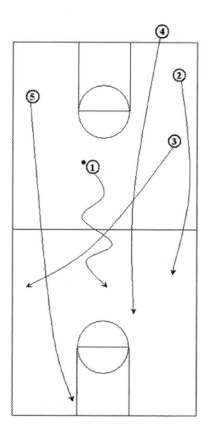

Get Together

Start of the break
Player 1 dribbles the ball down the court.
Player 2 fills the left lane.
Player 3 fills the right lane.
Player 5 goes to low post position.
Player 4 is the trailer.

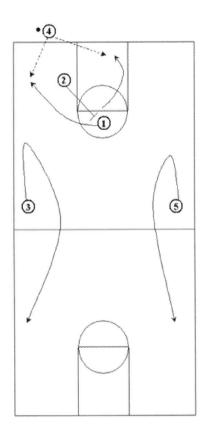

Roll 21

Players 3 and 5 begin to cut hard toward the ball executing a jab step and then sprints down to the three point line.

Player 2 back screens 1's defender then rolls to baseline looking for the pass, while 1 comes off the screen to ball side, at this point, 4 has option to hit 1 or 2.

Note: You must look and find the open man immediately, and making quick, accurate pass. Avoid soft, lob passes. Passing up the floor, and cutting, are the secrets to beating the press.

Look up the floor and anticipate where you will pass the ball, even before you set it. Any player receiving the ball wants to meet the pass – reducing the chance of a defender getting a hand on it – and simultaneously turn and square up in the Triple Threat position – which gives the player the option of a pass or a dribble.

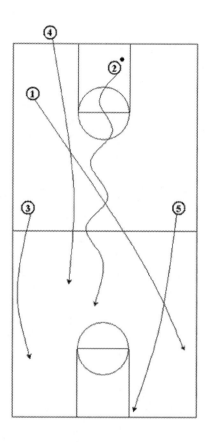

Roll 21

Start of the break
Player 2 pushes the ball down the court.
Players 3 and 1 fill the lanes.
Player 5 goes to low post position.
Player 4 is the trailer.

Note: If player 1 gets the inbound pass from 4, 2 takes the left lane.

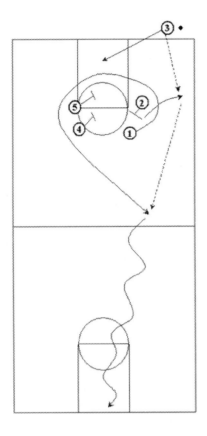

Circle

First Option

Player 2 bask screens for 1 then pops out to the ball side to get the
inbound pass from 3.

Player 1 loops around the double screen set by 4 and 5, heading to the
half-court line to get the ball from 2.

Player 1 pushes the ball down the court to attack the basket.

Note: This is simply a pattern that I used successfully in the past and can
be varied to suit the particular situation.

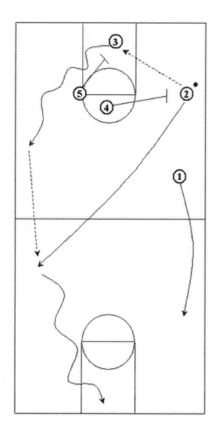

Circle

Second Option
If player 2 cannot pass to 1 then he reverses back to 3.
Player 4 screens for 2 and 5 ball screens for 3.
Player 3 will look ahead for 2, who cuts deep side for the pass.
Once player 2 gets the ball, he speed dribbles down the court to attack the basket.

Note: When 5 screens for 3, 3 has the options of passing to 2 or pushing the ball down the court.

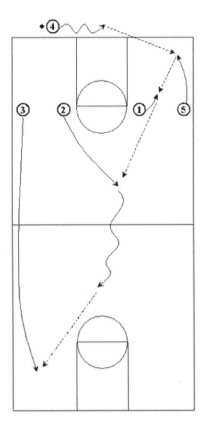

Line up

Here is a good press break to beat a full court defense man-to-man.

Player 4, the inbounder, runs baseline and hits 5 at corner, who immediately passes to 1.
Player 2 breaks to the middle of the press to receive the pass from 1.
Player 2 will push the ball down the court looking to create an opportunity to run a 2-on-1 break with 3.

Note: The best thing about this play is that by lining up your players at the beginning, it's much easier to inbound the ball against pressure. And the cutting afterwards really opens up the court, especially if you have a couple players that can really run and handle the ball.

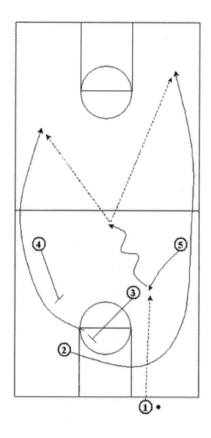

Scoring Thirty-Two

Here is a good press break to beat a full court defense man-to-man.

Player 3 sets a screen for 2, while 4 screens for 3.
Player 5 meets the inbound pass then advances the ball up the court while the wings run the outlet.
Player 5 looks to pass either to 3 or 2 for shot at the wings or drives all the way to the basket.

Full Court Zone
Press Breakers

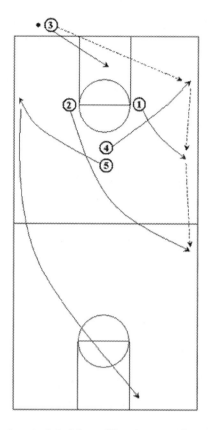

This play is highly effective against Full Court Zone Press 2-2-1,1-2-2 or any other zone press.

First Option
Players 4 and 5 start by breaking wide to the corners looking for ball.
Player 3 inbounds the ball to 4.
Player 4 immediately looks for 1 who pops out to the sideline to receive the ball.
Player 2 cuts deep sideline to get the pass from 1.
Player 5 sprints down the court to the ball side low block.

Note: If player 5 gets the inbound pass then 2 pops out to the sideline to get the pass from 5 and 1 cuts to deep sideline looking for ball from 2 and 4 sprints down the court to the ball side block.

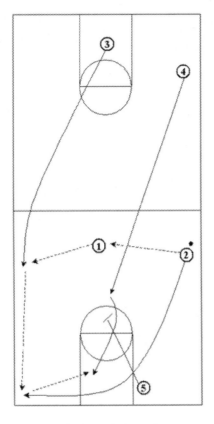

Here is a simple quick break.

Player 2 reverses the ball to 1 and cuts to the opposite corner.
Player 1 passes to 3.
Player 4 runs down the court to the top of the key.
Player 3 hits 2 at deep corner for a possible shot.
Player 5 up screens against 4's defender.
Player 4 cuts hard to the hoop to receive the pass from 2 for a shot in the lane or lay-up.

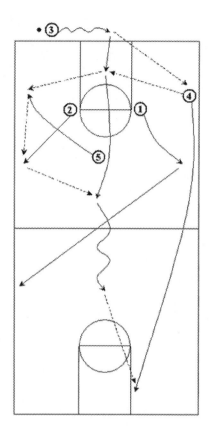

Reverse Pass
Second Option

If 4 cannot pass to 1 he then reverses to 3, who looks for 5 at the wing.
Player 5 gets the ball and quickly hits 2, who opens up to the sideline.
While 5 passes the ball to 2, 1 cuts deep sideline and 4 sprints down the
court to the mid-post position.
Player 3 sprints through the middle looking for a pass from 2.
If player 3 is open, 2 passes him the ball.
As they attack, 3 decides whether to go all the way to the hoop, shoot
from perimeter or pass to 4 for lay-up.

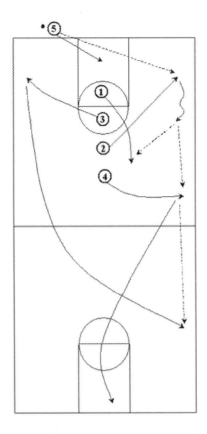

Middle Stack

Here is another simple play. The best way to beat a zone press is by getting the ball to the middle of the court and not dribble into any traps. Player 1 will be the main man in the middle of the court looking for the pass. This press break will work against most teams who use a zone press or man-to man.

First Option
At same time players 2 and 3 break to the wings to get the inbound pass from 5.
In this case 5 passes to 2.
When 2 catches the ball then 4 breaks near the half court line and 1 moves up to the middle.
Player 2 can pass either to 1 in the middle or 4 over the top if any traps occur.

96

Remember that player 4 will try to get free for the pass over the top of any trap made at half-court against 2.

If player 4 gets the ball, he looks to pass to 3 at the deep sideline.

If player 3 gets the ball he looks for 4 cutting to the basket.

If player 1 gets the ball from 2, then 1 advances the ball down the court to attack the basket.

Player 5 is the trailer, 2 and 3 fill the lanes and 4 goes to ball side low block.

Note: When receiving the inbounds pass, catch it and get into triple-threat position facing the defense and look up the floor before immediately starting your dribble. Look up the court. Don't look down at the ball. Don't dribble unless you have to. You beat the press by quick, sharp passing usually not dribbling

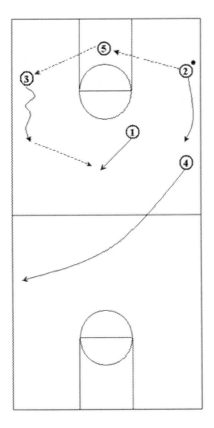

Middle Stack - Reverse Pass

Second Option
If player 2 gets the double team and he cannot pass to 1 or 4 he then reverses the ball to 5 the trailer.
Player 5 quickly passes the ball to 3.
When 3 receives the pass, his intention is to dribble down the court to beat the press or looks for 1 at middle to see if he is open.
It is good to know that 1 should look for gaps in the press and get between the defenders to make the catch.
Player 4 flashes to the opposite sideline for a possible pass from 3 or 1.

Note: Sometimes 2 or 3 will be able to use a speed dribble to beat the trap at half-court, but if you can get the ball to the middle against zone press you can beat it easily.

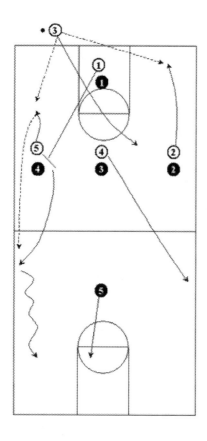

Press Beak Against 1-3-1
One Up

Player 2 starts the play by breaking to the baseline asking for ball.
Player 1 back screen against 5's defender and pops out to the sideline.
Player 3 quickly inbounds to 5 and 5 reverse to 1.
Player 1 attacks the basket.
If player 2 gets the inbound pass he can either dribble the ball down the court or hits 3 at mid-court to start the break.
Player 4 goes deep.

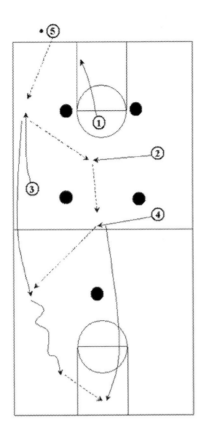

Press Break Against 2-2-1

Here is a good quick break play in the last second situation of the game when your opponent introduces a 2-2-1 full court zone press.

First Option
Player 1 breaks toward the ball, while 3 comes up to meet the pass.
Player 5, the inbouder, fakes pass to 1 but instead makes a quick pass up the side to 3.
As the defense attempts to trap 3, 2 cuts hard to the middle looking for a pass from 3.
Player 2 catches the ball and quickly looks for 4 who flashes from behind the defense to get the pass at center court.
Player 4 immediately outlets to 3, who attacks the basket.
Player 3 drives to the hoop to draw the defender and looks to feed 4 for lay-up.

100

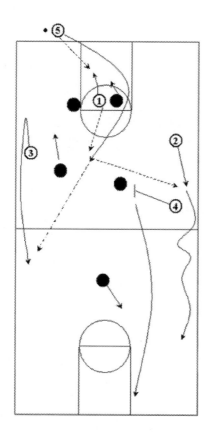

Press Break Against 2-2-1
Second Option

Player 1 breaks toward the inbounder, 5, to receive the ball.
 Player 5, after inbounds the ball to 1, quickly does a semicircle to receive the ball back from 1 in the middle of the zone.
This movement from 5 creates an outlet pass either to 2 or 3.
In this case player 2 gets the ball and 4 will back screen the nearest defender, providing 2 an easy trip down the court.
Player 4 sprints to the ball side block and we are in offense.

Remember: When player 5 catches the ball, his objective is to outlet quickly to 2 or 3. As you see this play creates a two against one situation at the basket.

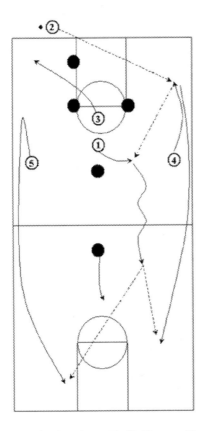

Press Break Against Full Court Zone Press 1-2-1-1
First Option

Player 3 attempted to get the ball from 2, the inbounder, by breaking toward the corner to draw the defenders.
Player 4 flashes to the weakside wing to get the inbound pass from 2.
Player 4 immediately hits 1 at the mid-court.
Player 1 pushes the ball down the court looking for 5 or 4 cutting to the basket for lay-up.

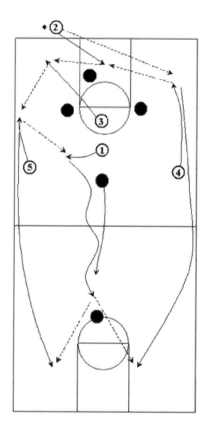

Press Break Against 1-2-1-1 – Reverse Pass
Second Option

If the pass is denied against 1, then 4 quickly reverse the ball to 2 and 2
hits 3 at the wing.
Player 5 comes up to meet the pass from 3 and hits 1 at mid-court.
Players 4 and 5 run the lanes.
Player 1 pushes the ball down the court looking for 4 or 5 for a one-on-
one situation at the hoop.

Note: Look for good shots and do not play into the defense's hands by
taking quick or rushed shots. One of the goals of a press or trap is to
speed up play -- it is important to take your time and find a good open
shot.

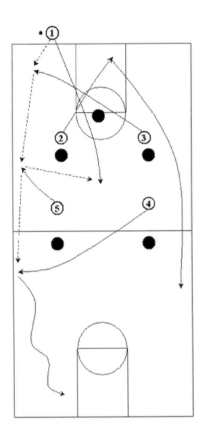

Press Break Against 1-2-2
First Option

Player 2 begins with a simple cut through the lane looking for the pass.
Player 3 breaks to the ball side short corner to receive the inbound pass from 1.
Player 5 comes up to get the pass from 3, while 1 runs up to the mid-court looking for possible pass from 5.
Player 5 can either pass to 1, starting the offense (fast break), or 4 who flashes deep sideline to release the pressure.
Player 4 can either attack the basket or hand off to 1 to initiate half-court offense.

Note: Position one player in the middle of the floor at all times. This forces the defense to defend the middle, which is one of the most vulnerable areas of the 1-2-2.

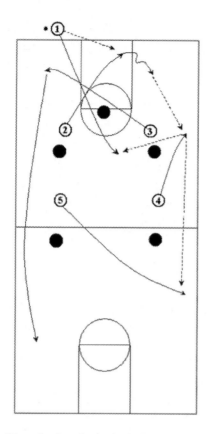

Press Break Against 1-2-2
Second Option

If player 1 decides to inbound pass to 2, then 4 comes up to meet the pass at wing. At the same time 1 runs up to the mid-court and 5 flashes deep sideline, both are open for the pass from 4.

If player 1 gets the ball then he pushes the ball down the court to start the break with 3 and 5.

If 5 receives the ball either he attacks the basket or hands off to 1 to initiate half-court offense.

Note: Position one player deep so the defense has to respect and cover him, forcing their defense to spread more and create more openings. Your last player should work the sideline or wing area on the opposite side of the court from the deep man. This ensures that one defender cannot guard both of those players.

Practice; practice is the key.

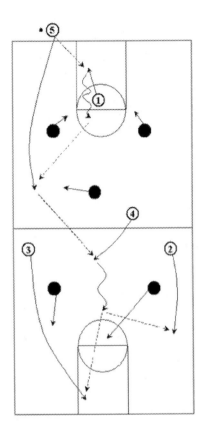

Press Break Against 2-1-2
First Option

This is a simple press break with a single pass to 5 to beat the press.

Player 1 cuts toward the inbouder, 5, to receive the ball.

Player 1 dribbles down court to draw the front line defenders.

Player 5 sprints up the side to receive the reverse pass from 1.

This movement from 5 will avoid 1 from being trapped.

When 5 gets the ball, he quickly looks for 4, who flashes to the middle.

Player 4 catches the ball then dribbles to the top of the key looking for 3 cutting to basket, or 2 at the wing for a shot.

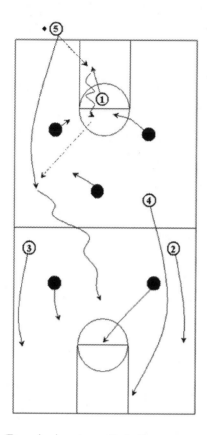

Press Break Against 2-1-2
Second Option

Here is another away to beat this press very quickly.
In this option, player 5 gets the ball and dribbles all the way to top of key
looking to pass to either: 2, 3 or 4 to attack the basket.

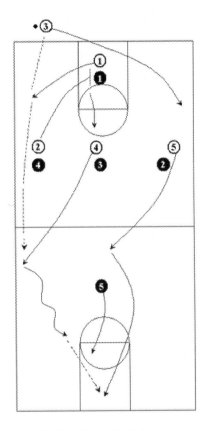

Press Break Against 1-3-1
Petra Step One

Player 2 screens against 1's defender then opens up to the middle of the
court while 1 breaks to the ballside wing to get the inbound pass.
Player 4 goes deep sideline looking for the over head pass from 1.
If player 4 gets the ball he will drive to the hoop or lob to 5 for a dunk.

Note: When player 2 screens against 1's defender it will take away the
double trap.   If defender X3 follows 4 then 1 can advance the ball down
the court. Good quick passes will break the press.

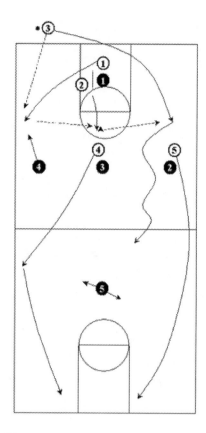

Petra Reverse
Step Two

If player 1 decides to pass to the middle of the zone, in this case to 2,
Player 2 advances down the court or passes to 3 who is wide open.
This should be a fast, easy break between 2 or 3, one of them should
find 4 or 5 to score.

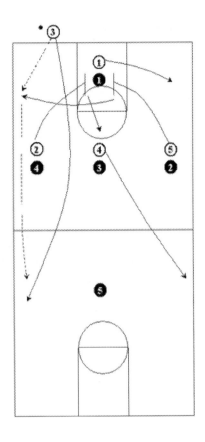

Press Break Against 1-3-1
Akaba
Option One

At same time players 2 and 5 screen against 1's defender then 5 cuts toward the ball.
Player 3 inbounds the ball to 5, then runs down sideline to receive the over head pass from 5.
The press is beaten.
Players 3 and 4 should be able to attack the basket.

Note: If player 5 cannot pass to 3 then he looks for 2 at the middle to beat the press.

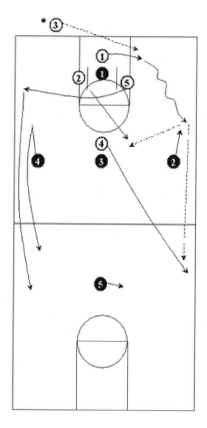

Akaba

Option Two

Player 3 inbounds the ball to 1.

Player X2 will close out against 1.

Player 4 goes deep sideline looking to get the pass from 1.

Player 1 can either pass to 4 or 2 at the middle.

If player 2 gets the ball he then brings the ball down to attack the basket with 5 and 4.

Player 3 stays back as safety option.

Note: If player 4 gets the ball he will drive to the basket looking to lob pass to 5 for a dunk.

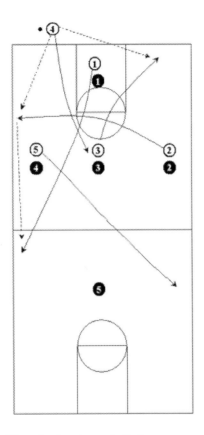

Press Break Against 1-3-1
Madaba

Player 1 starts the play by breaking deep to right sideline.
Player 3 drops to baseline and 2 crosses toward the ball to get the
inbound pass from 4. Player 5 goes deep and 4 cuts high to the middle.
If player 2 passes to 1, then the press is beaten immediately.
If player 4 decides to pass to 3 then 3 brings the ball down the court or
looks to 4 in the middle or 5 at the deep sideline.

Note: When player 2 gets the inbound pass, his primary objective is to
get the ball to 1 to break the press quickly.

Baseline Out-of-Bounds
Last Second Plays

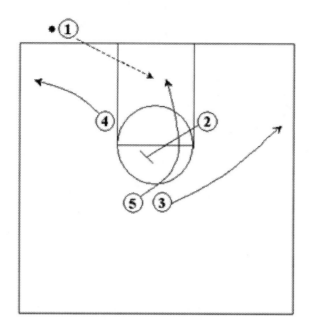

One Second Remaining

Player 4 pops out to the ball side corner. He must take his defensive man away from the basket.

Player 3 breaks to the three point area opposite of the ball.

Player 2 has to search hard for X5 as he sets a diagonal screen for 5.

Player 5 comes off the screen into the lane to receive a lob pass from 1 for a dunk.

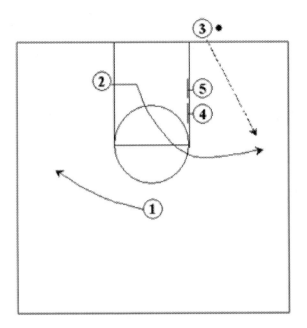

Two Seconds Remaining

Player 1 breaks hard to the three-point line on the left wing.
Player 2 v-cuts toward the ball and then curls off the double screen set
by 4 and 5 for a quick shot.

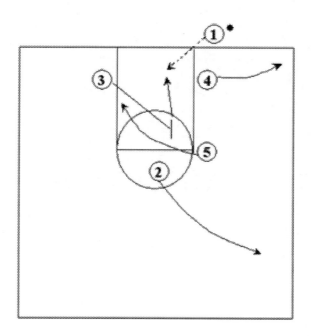

Two Seconds Remaining

Player 2 goes higher than the free-throw line extended.
Player 4 step-slides away from the basket asking for the ball.
Player 3 sets a diagonal screen for 5 and rolls to the basket to receive an inbound pass from 1 for a shot in the lane.

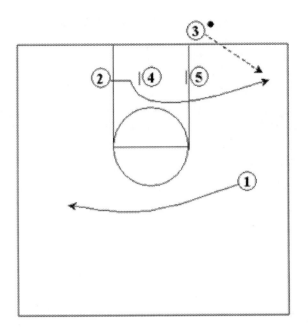

Two Seconds Remaining

Player 1 breaks to opposite wing.

Players 4 and 5 set a staggered screen for 2.

Player 2 gets inbound pass from 3 at ball side corner for a shot.

Note: If player 2 cannot get the inbound pass, then player 3 looks to pass to 5 who tries to pin the defender and receive a lob pass.

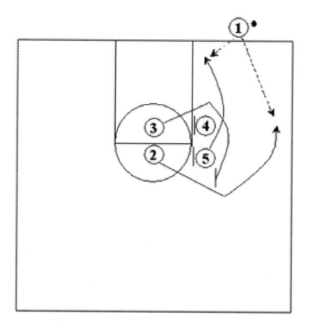

Two Seconds Remaining

Player 3 begins by curling around 4 to screen with 5 against 2's defender.
Player 2 comes off a double screen to the ball side wing and at the same time, 5 cuts hard to the ball.
Player 1 can hit 2 at wing or 5 at low post for a shot.

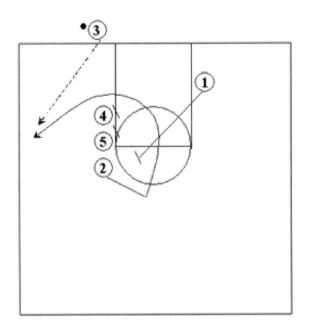

Two Seconds Remaining

Player 1 sets a diagonal screen against 2's defender.
Player 2 comes off the single screen set by 1 and wraps around the double screen set by 4 and 5 to the ball side corner.
Player 3 inbounds a pass to 2 for a baseline jumper.

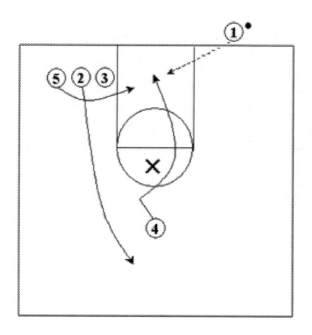

One Second Remaining

Player 2 flashes to the top of key.

Player 3 screens for 5.

Player 5 pretends to cut into the lane to distract 4's defender, while 4 executes a v-cut and explodes to the hoop to receive a lob pass from 1 for a dunk.

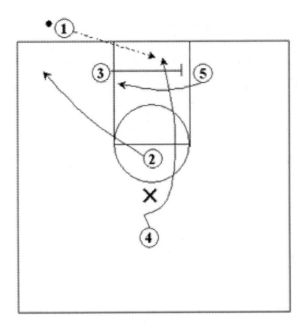

One Second Remaining

Player 2 breaks to deep corner yelling for ball.

Player 5 sets up his defender and cuts hard off 3's screen toward the ball.
At the same time player 4 V-cuts and sprints hard into the lane looking
for a lob pass from 1 for a dunk.

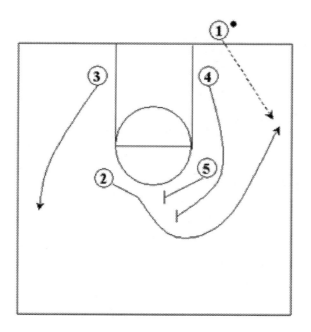

Two Seconds Remaining

Player 3 pops out to the left wing.

Player 4 sets an up-screen with 5 against 2's defender.

Player 2 comes off a double screen to the ball side wing to receive an inbound pass from 1 for a quick shot.

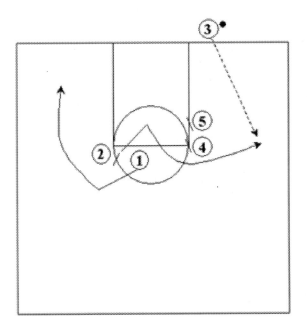

Two Seconds Remaining

Player 2 back screens for 1.
Then player 2 comes off the double screen, set by 4 and 5, to receive an inbound pass from 3 for a shot.

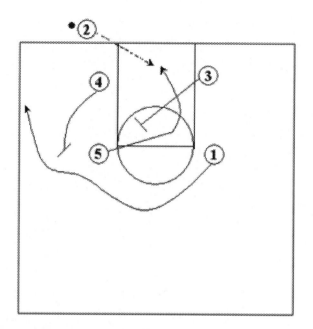

One Second Remaining

Player 1 starts by cutting to the ball side wing to receive a screen by 4. While player 1 cuts to the ball side, player 3 sets a solid back screen for 5. Player 5 explodes into the lane to receive an inbound pass from 2 for a dunk.

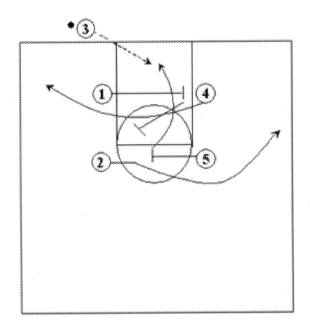

One Second Remaining

Player 5 screens for 2.

Player 1 cross-screens for 4 and then back screens against 5's defender.

Player 5 cuts hard to the rim looking for a lob pass from 3 for a dunk.

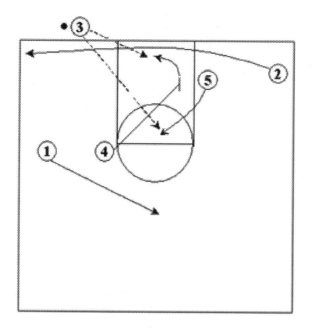

One Second Remaining

Player 2 begins by cutting to the ball side corner.

Player 1 moves to the top of the key.

Player 4 screens for 5 and pins low.

Player 3 looks to lob pass to either 5 or 4 for a quick shot.

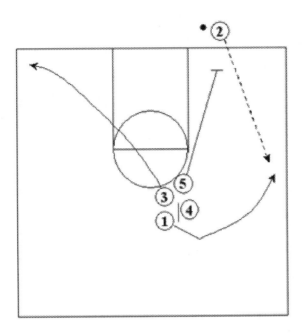

Two Seconds Remaining

Set the players at foul lane extended.

All players move at the same time when 2 slaps the ball.

Player 3 clears out to the left corner.

Player 5 down screens 2's defender at baseline.

Player 4 sets a back screen for 1 at top of the key.

Player 1 cuts off the screen to receive an inbound pass from 2 on the wing for a 3 point shot.

Baseline Out-of-Bounds Against 2-3 Zone Defense Last Seconds

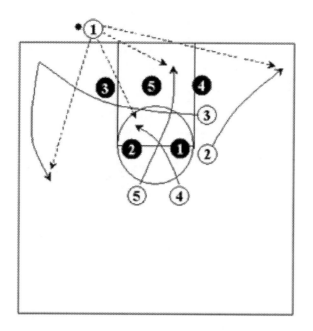

Last Seconds Against 2-3 Zone Defense
All Ball

When inbounder slaps the ball, all players move at the same time.
Player 2 breaks to the right corner.
Player 3 cuts to the ball side corner then pivots quickly up to wing.
Player 5 cuts through the middle of the zone and 4 cuts across the lane.

Options: Player 1 can hit 2 at corner, 5 inside the box, 3 at wing or 4 coming across the lane.

Note: This is an excellent play against 2-3 zone – all your players have to move at the same time ready for the pass.

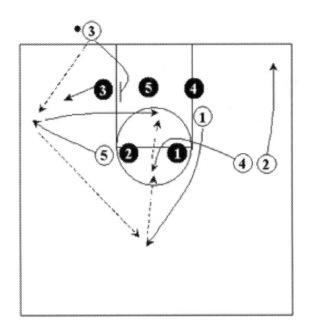

Fast Five

Player 5 pops out from the elbow to the ball side to get the inbound pass from 3.

Player 1 steps hard and high to receive the pass from 5.

Player 2 slides down to the corner.

Player 4 flashes to the free throw line to get the ball from 1

Player 3 steps to the block and sets a back screen against X3.

Player 4 passes to 5, who cuts hard to basket for a shot.

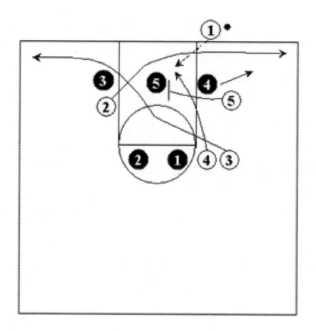

43 Down

Players 2 and 3 cut to opposite corners.
Player 5 screens the middle of the zone defender against X5.
The actions of 2 and 5 open up the lane for 4 to receive the inbound
pass from 1 for a shot under the basket.

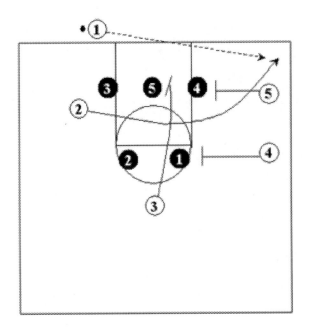

Wall 54

Player 3 cuts through the lane to screen the middle zone against X5.

At the same time 4 screens X1 and 5 screens X4.

Player 2 cuts off double screen to the corner.

Player 1 inbounds to 2 for a quick turn-around jump shot.

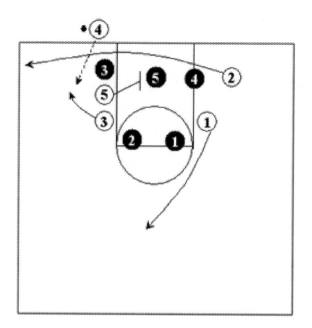

Eye Ball

Player 2 cuts to the ball side corner and 1 steps up high.
Player 5 screens the middle of the zone against X5.
Player 3 pops out toward the ball for a shot.

Note: When 2 cuts to the corner X3, the defender, will closeout against 2 and open up the baseline for a shot.

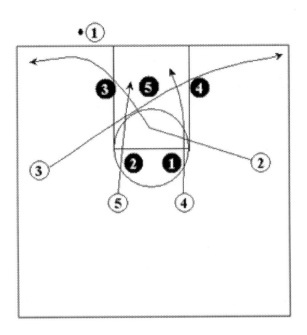

Get It

Players move all at once.

Players 2 and 3 cut through the lane to opposite corners.

While 2 and 3 scatter to the corners, 4 cuts into the lane and 5 follows right behind looking for an opening in the middle.

Player 1, inbounder, looks to pass to either 5 or 4 in the box.

Sideline Out-of-Bounds
Last Second Plays

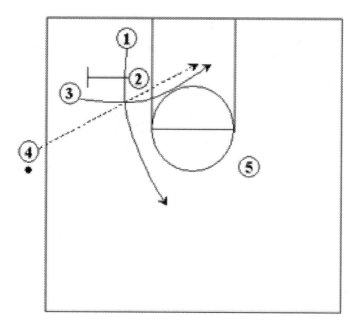

One Second Remaining

Player 1 flashes to the top of the key with intention of getting the ball. At same time player 2 sets a solid back screen for 3, who comes off the screen, to the hoop to receive a lob pass from 4, for a catch in the air and tip in.

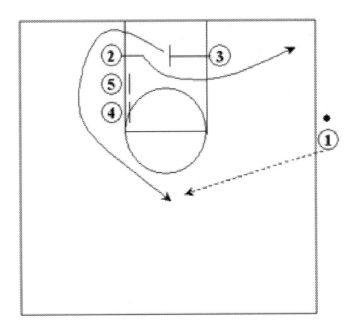

Two Seconds Remaining

Player 3 cross-screens for 2 who cuts to the ball side corner looking for the ball.
Players 4 and 5 set a double screen for 3.
Player 3 breaks to the three-point area to receive an inbound pass from 1 for a shot.

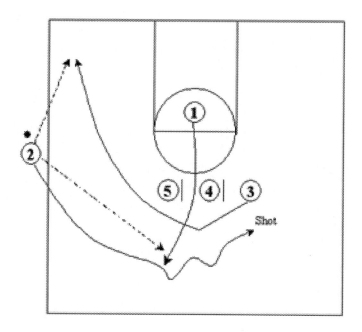

Three Seconds Remaining

Players 4 and 5 set staggered screens for 3, who cuts to the ball side looking for ball.

Player 1 breaks to the top of the key to receive inbound pass from 2.

Player 2 steps in to receive a hand-off from 1.

Player 2 dribbles away from 1 to the three point line for a jump shot.

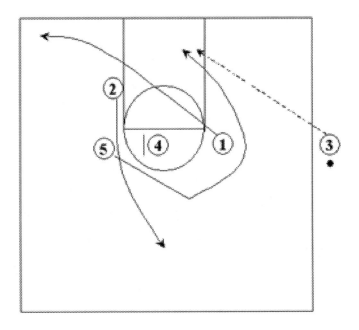

Two Seconds Remaining

Player 1 breaks to the opposite corner.

Player 2 comes up to the top of the key asking for ball.

Player 4 sets a solid back screen for 5.

Player 5 comes off the screen down the lane to receive the pass from 3 for lay-up.

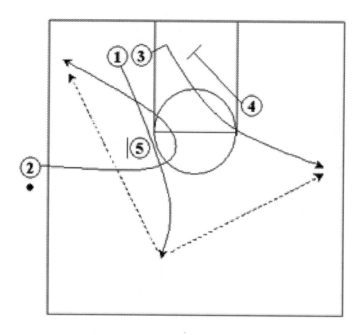

Four Seconds Remaining

Player 1 flashes to the top of the key to get an inbound pass from 2.
Player 2 passes to 1 and wraps around 5 to the ball side deep corner.
At same time player 4 sets down screen for 3 who cuts to the three point line.
Player 1 can look to pass to 2 or 3 for a quick shot.

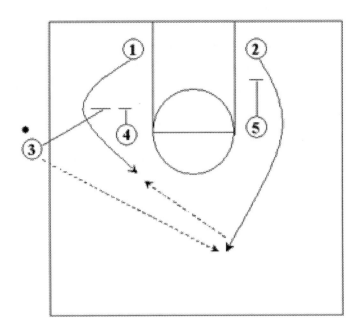

Four Seconds Remaining

Player 5 down screens for 2.

Player 3 inbound pass to 2.

Player 3 steps in to set a double screen with 4 for 1.

Player 1 comes off the double screen to receive a pass from 2 for a shot.

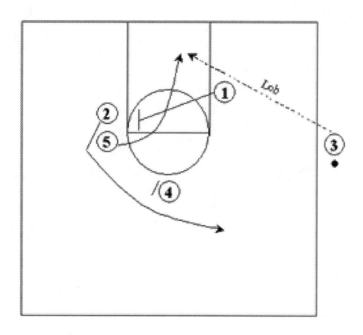

One Second Remaining

Player 4 sets a screen for 2.
Player 1 back screens 5's defender.
Player 5 explodes to the hoop to receive a lob pass from 3 for a dunk.

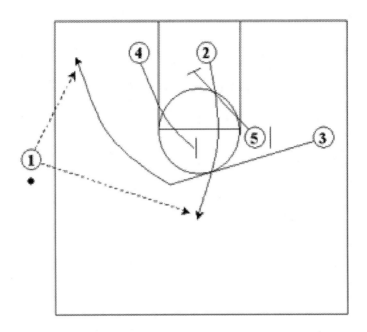

Two Seconds Remaining

Player 4 comes up to set a staggered screen with 5 for 3.

Player 3 comes off the screens to the ball side corner.

Player 5, after screening for 3, sets a down screen for 2 who steps hard and high.

Player 1 looks to inbound pass to 3, 2 or 5 who tries to seal his defender in the lane.

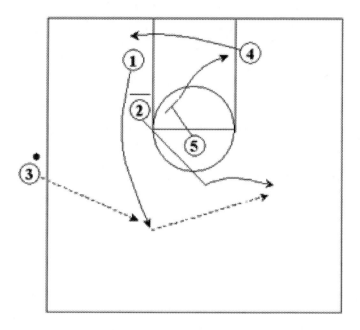

Four Seconds Remaining

Player 2 down screens for 1 and player 4 clears out to the ball side block.
Player 1 cuts hard and high to get an inbound pass from 3.
Player 5 back screens for 2 then cuts to the right block.
Player 2 comes off the screen to receive the ball from 1 for a pull-up jump shot at three point line.

Note: If player 2 cannot shoot then he looks for 5 in low post area.

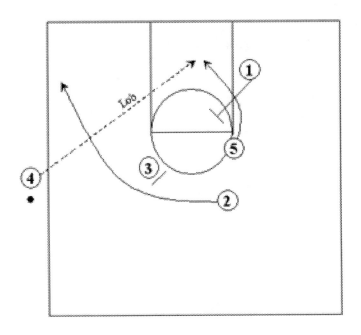

One Second Remaining

Player 3 sets a pick for 2.
Player 2 cuts to the ball side corner.
Player 1 back screens 5's defender.
Player 5 cuts hard to the hoop looking for a lob pass from 4 for a dunk.

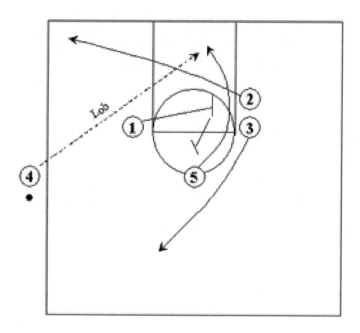

One Second Remaining

Player 1 screens for 2, who cuts to the ball side corner.

Player 3 steps hard and high asking for ball.

Player 1, after screens for 2, then back screens 5's defender.

Player 5 cuts hard to the basket looking for a lob pass from 4 for a dunk.

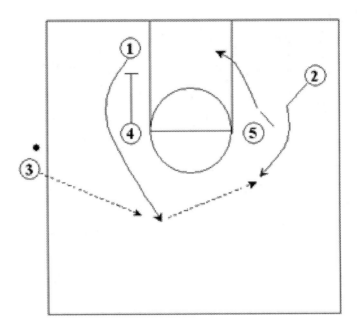

Three Seconds Remaining

Player 4 down screens for 1.

Player 3 inbound pass to 1.

Player 5 sets a solid screen for 2 then rolls to the basket.

Player 2 comes off the screen to receive a pass from 1 for a quick shot.

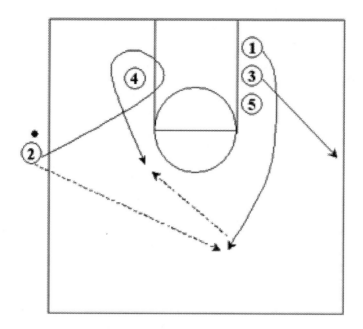

Four Seconds Remaining

Player 1 cuts high to receive inbound pass from 2.
Player 3 pops out to the wing.
Player 2, after inbound pass to 1, then loops around 4 to get the reverse pass from 1 for a quick shot at foul line extended.

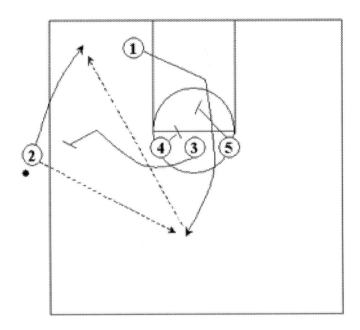

Three Seconds Remaining

Player 5 down screens for 1.

Player 1 cuts hard and high to receive inbound pass from 2.

Player 4 screens for 3, who then back screens 2's defender.

Player 2 steps into the corner to receive the over head pass from 1 for a shot.

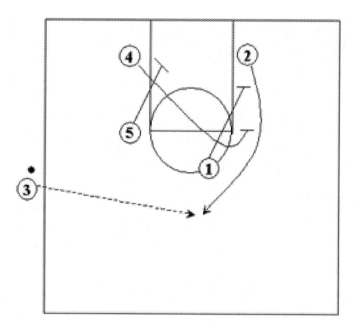

Two Seconds Remaining

Player 5 down screens for 4, and 4 comes up to set staggered screen with 1 for 2.

Player 2 comes up to receive an inbound pass from 3 for a quick shot at three point line.

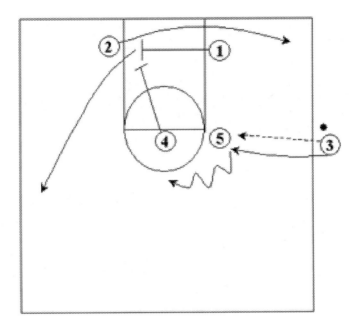

Two Seconds Remaining

Player 3 is the shooter.

Player 1 cross-screens for 2 while 2 cuts to the ball side corner looking for a pass.

Player 4 down screens for 1, so we pick the picker.

Player 1 sprints to the wing "calling for ball".

Player 3, inbound pass to 5 at elbow, then immediately steps in to receive the hand off from 5 for a pull-up jump shot.

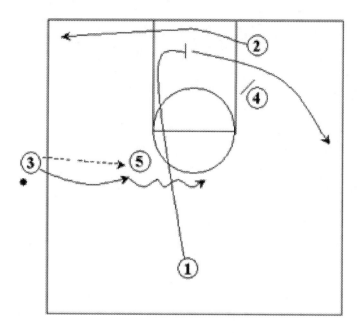

Two Seconds Remaining

Player 1 cuts through the lane to screen for 2 at the same time player 4 screens for 1.
Player 3 inbounds to 5 at elbow, then steps in to receive the hand off from 5 for a jump shot at three point line.

Note: Player 3's first option is to look for 2 at corner.

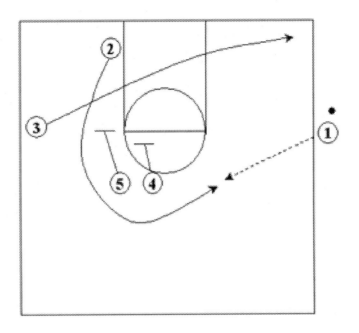

Two Seconds Remaining

Player 3 breaks to the ball side corner.
Player 2 sprints up to receive a double screen set by 4 and 5 for a quick shot at three point area.

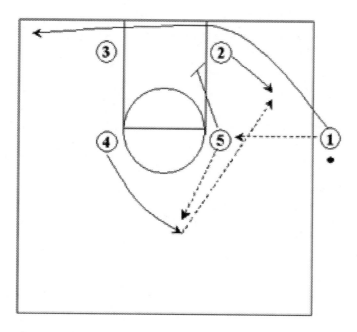

Four Seconds Remaining

Player 1 inbound pass to 5 at elbow and cuts baseline to the ball side corner.

Player 4 pops out to the top of the key to receive the pass from 5.

Player 5 down screens for 2.

Player 2 comes off the screen to the short corner- to receive the ball from 4 for a pull-up jump shot.

Sideline Out-of-Bounds Against 2-3 Zone Defense

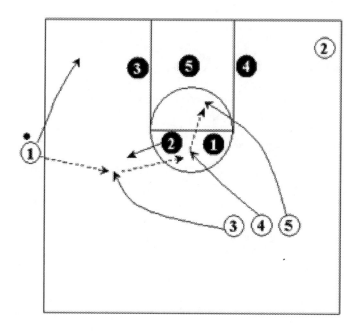

Zone Offense Side-line Out-Bounds Last Seconds
345 Top

Player 3 comes to the ball to receive the inbound pass from 1 and
quickly passes to 4 who cuts to the nail.
Remember that when player 3 gets the ball, X2 will come out against 3
and opens up a gap for 4 to get the pass.
Player 5 flashes through the middle of the zone to receive the pass from
4 for a shot in the lane.

Note: If X4 closeout against 5, then 5 looks to pass to 2 at corner for a
three-point shot.

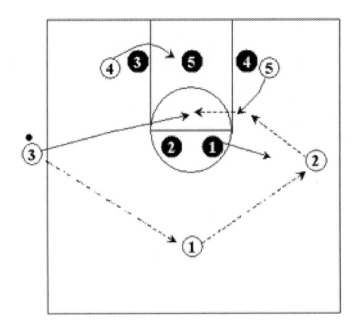

Five Up

Player 3 inbound pass to 1 and 1 swings 2 at right wing.
Player 5 comes up to the high post to receive the pass from 2 and quickly hits 3 who flashes into the middle of the lane for a shot.

Note: When 3 receives the ball, player 4 cuts behind the zone for a possible pass from 3 for a shot under the basket.

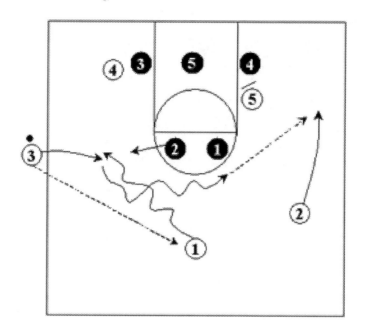

Open Two

Player 3 inbound pass to 1.

Player 1 dribbles towards X2 and hands off to 3.

Player 3 dribbles into the gap between X2 and X1 and hits 2 at wing for a three-point shot.

Note: X1 defender should come out to stop the dribble penetration against 3 and for that 2 will be wide open at wing.

Player 5 should seal his defender X4 at low post block.

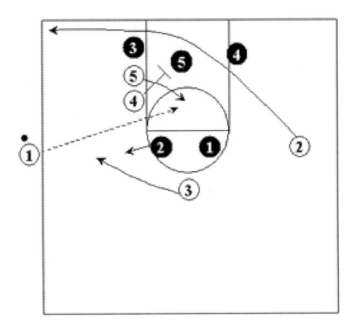

Lob Five

Player 2 cuts to the ball side corner.
Player 3 breaks toward the ball.
Player 4 screens the middle of the zone against X5 defender, that leaves
5 totally free to position himself in the box for a lob pass from 1 for
hook shot.

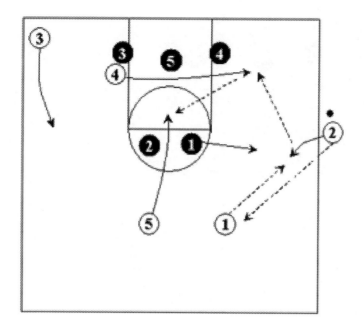

Five Inn

Player 2 inbound pass to 1 and 1 reverses to 2 at wing.
Player 4 cuts across the lane to the ball side to receive the ball from 2.
Player 5 who is at top of the key dives into the middle of the lane to receive a pass from 4 for a shot.

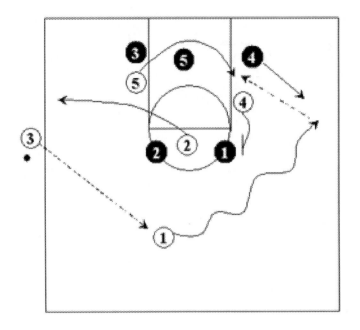

Man Entry

Player 2 breaks toward the ball looking for the pass.

Player 3 inbound pass to 1.

Player 4 back screens the top of the zone X1 defender.

Player 1 dribbles to the right wing looking to pass to 5 who cuts behind the zone to the ball side low post block for a shot.

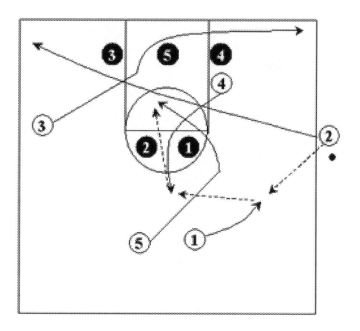

Boys Shuffle

Player 2 inbound pass to 1.

At the same time players 2 and 3 cut to opposite corners.

Player 4 steps high to get the ball from 1.

Player 5 cuts into the lane looking for the pass from 4 for a shot in the box.

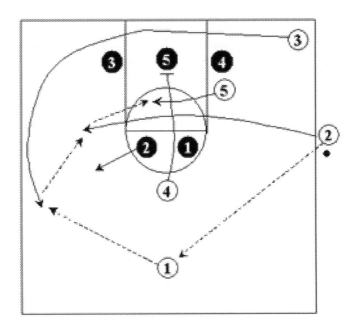

Down Four

Player 2 begins with an inbound pass to 1.

Player 3 breaks to opposite wing to receive the ball from 1, while 2 cuts toward 3 to meet the pass.

When 2 catches the ball, 4 down screens in the middle of the zone allowing 5 to flash into the box to receive the ball from 2 for a quick shot.

Full Court Last-Second Plays

"Buzzer Beaters"

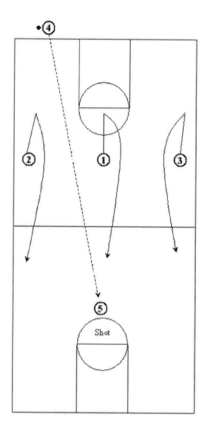

Rocket

One Second Remaining

Players 1, 2 and 3 begin to take a couple steps toward the ball and then back-cut to the three-point-arc.

While players come at the ball, player 2 throws a long pass for 5 to catch-and-shoot in the air.

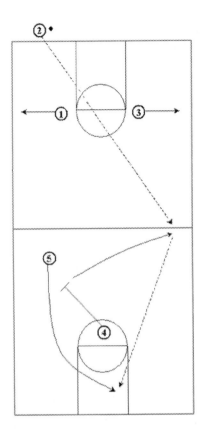

Out 13
Three Seconds Remaining

Player 1 and 3 split sides of the court.
Player 4 back screens for 5 and pops out to receive the long pass from 2 at mid-court line.
Player 5 cuts diagonally to the basket to receive a pass from 4 for a shot in the box.

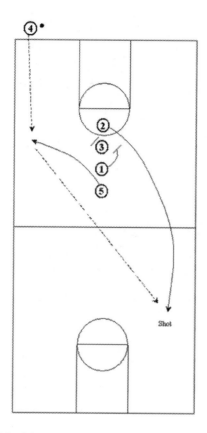

Quickly Two
Three Seconds Remaining

Player 4 is your best passer.

Player 5 pops out to the ball side to get the inbound pass from 4.

Quickly, 5 catches the ball and looks for 2 who will get screen set by 3 and 1.

Player 2 sprints down the court near the three point line for a pull-up jump shot.

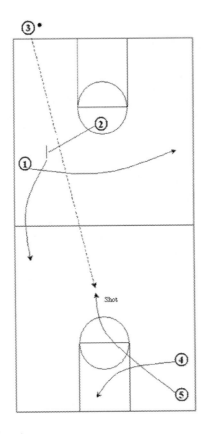

Flash Five
One Second Remaining

Distraction and pretending is what this play is all about.
Player 2 screens for 1.
At same time, player 4 cuts to the basket and 5 flashes to the top of the key to receive a long pass from 3 for a quick shot.

Note: Practice this shot movement twice a week at end of your practice.

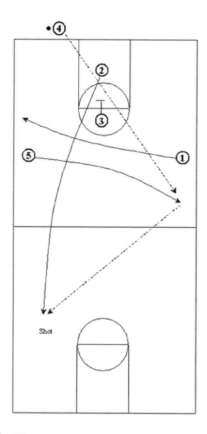

Bomb Two

Three Seconds Remaining

Player 2 is your best shooter.

Simple as that, players 1 and 5 cut to opposite sides of the court to confuse the defenders.

Player 1 asks for ball.

Player 3 down screens for 2.

Player 5 gets the inbound pass.

While 5 catches the ball player 2 sprints down the court looking for the pass from 5 for a quick jump shot.

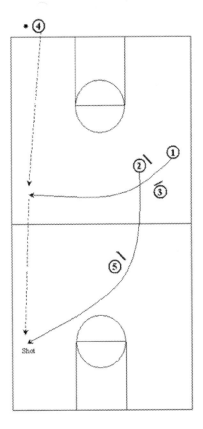

Over Load

Three Seconds Remaining

Place all your players at one side of the court.

Player 2 screens for 1.

Player 5 screens for 2.

Player 4 inbound pass to 1 at half court.

Player 1 passes the ball to 2 for a quick shot.

Note: Make sure player 5 sets a solid screen against 2's defender.

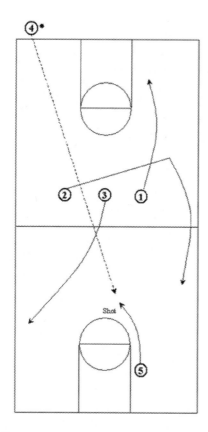

231 Up
One Second Remaining

Line up your players 2, 3 and 1 near half court line.
Start with player 2 by cutting to opposite side of the court.
Then player 3 slides down to the ball side asking for ball.
Player 5 flashes to the top of the key.
Player 4 inbound pass to 5 for a turn-around shot.

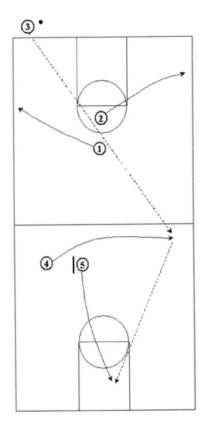

Wide Boys
Three Seconds Remaining

Simple play and very effective.
Players 1 and 2 break to opposite sides of the court.
Player 5 sets a pick for 4 and rolls to the basket.
Player 3 inbound pass to 4.
Player 4 hits 5 in the lane.
Player 5 goes for a quick shot under the basket.

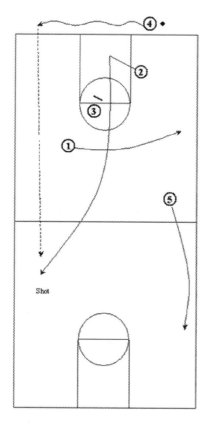

Catches and Shoot.

Two Seconds Remaining

Player 1 breaks to the ball side.

Player 4, the inbounder, runs baseline looking for 2 who gets a screen by 3.

Player 2 catches the ball and shoots.

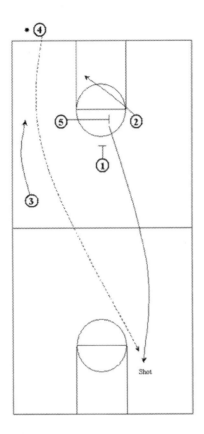

Long Ball Five
Two Seconds Remaining

Player 3 cuts toward the ball.
Player 5 fakes a screen for 2 and gets screen by 1.
Player 5 runs down the court to receive the long pass from 4 for a shot near the basket.

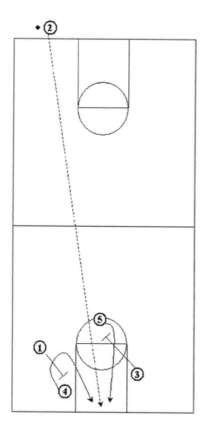

Inside
One Second Remaining

This is for a desperate situation of the game when you have only one second to survive.
Place all your players around the box.
At same time, player 1 down screens for 4 and 3 back screens for 5.
Player 2 throws the ball close to the rim.
Both big players crash to the rim to catch the ball up in the air and tip in.

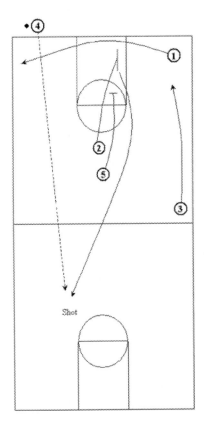

52 UP

Two Seconds Remaining

Player 3 breaks to the baseline.

Player 2 sets a pick for 1 who cuts toward the inbounder asking for ball.

Player 5 sets a solid down screen for 2.

Player 2 sprints down the court looking for a long pass from 4 for a shot.

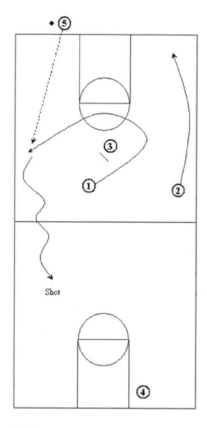

Up and Fast
Three Seconds Remaining

Player 2 starts the play by cutting toward the baseline and call for ball.
At same time player 3 back screens 1's defender.
Player 1 comes off the the screen looping to ball side to receive the
inbound pass from 5.
Player 1 quickly pushes the ball down the court for a quick shot.

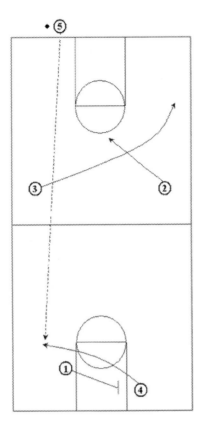

Throw Me
One Second Remaining

Player 2 cuts to the top of the key.
Player 3 breaks to the opposite wing.
Player 1 baseline cross screen for 4.
Player 4 comes off the screen to receive the inbound pass from 5.
Player 4 catch-and-shoot in the air.

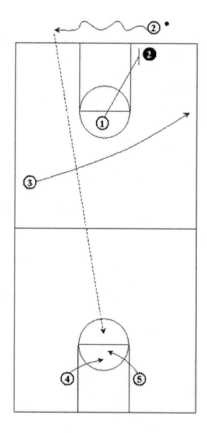

Run

One Second Remaining

This is a play to catch and shoot.

Player 3 starts the play by cutting to the ball side wing asking for ball.

Player 1 screens 2's defender at baseline.

Player 2, the inbounder, runs baseline to opposite direction and throws a long pass to 4 or 5.

Whoever receives the ball will catch-and-shoot in the air.

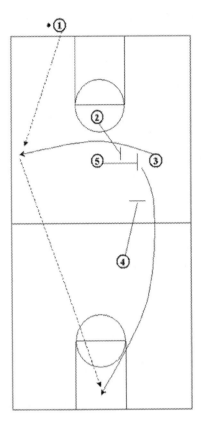

Bomb

Three Seconds Remaining

Players 2 and 5 double screen for 3.

Player 3 cuts to the ball side to get the inbound pass from 1.

Player 4 sets a blind screen on 5's defender.

Player 5 sprints down the court looking to receive the pass from 3 for a shot in the lane.

Note: If player 3 cannot pass to 5 he then attempts to shoot the ball quickly from the half court line to the basket.

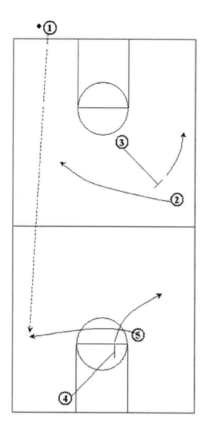

Ladder

Two Seconds Remaining

Player 3 back screens for 2 then pops out to the wing.
Player 2 comes off the screen pretending to get the ball.
At the same time 4 back screens for 5 who flashes to the ball side wing.
Player 1 looks to pass to 5 for a quick shot.

Note: The inbounder should look for the deep pass first, if the pass is not available then players 2 and 3 should be able to get the ball and shoot.

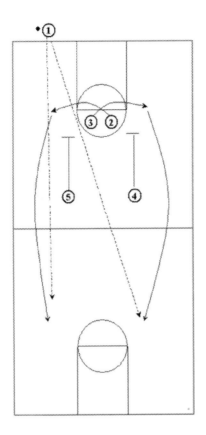

Cross 32
Two Seconds Remaining

Players 3 and 2 position themselves at free throw line then cross over.
Player 4 screens for 3 and 5 screens for 2.
Players 3 and 2 use the screens and sprint wide looking for a deep pass
over the top of the defense for a shot.

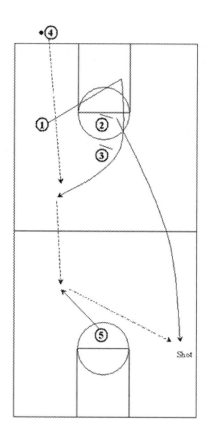

Loop

Four Seconds Remaining

Player 1 cuts through the lane, receiving a staggered screen by 2 and 3.
Player 1 loops around them to the middle of the court looking for pass
from 4.

Player 3 screens 2's defender while 2 sprints down the court to the left
wing, 5 comes up toward half-court line to receive the pass from 1.

Player 5 catches the ball and quickly hits 2 for a jump shot.

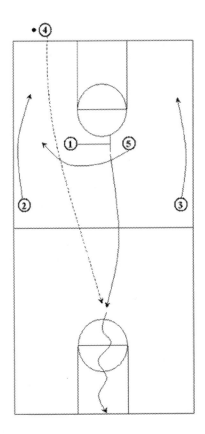

Flash One
Three Seconds Remaining

Players 2 and 3 cut toward baseline asking for ball.
Player 1 sets a screen for 5 then sprints down the court to receive a long
pass from 4 for lay-up.

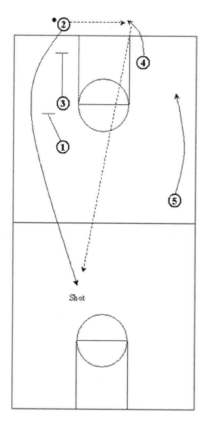

Man Switch
Two Seconds Remaining

As player 2 receives the ball from the official, player 4 steps out of bounds.

Player 2 throws the ball to 4 (out bounds) and receives a set screen by players 3 and 1.

Player 2 is free to sprint down court to receive a long pass from 4 for a shot.

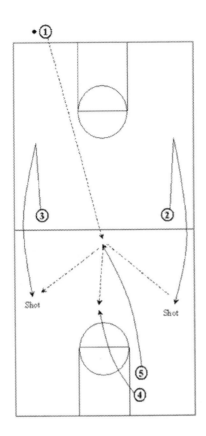

32 Down
Four Seconds Remaining

Players 3 and 2 start to cut toward the ball executing a jab step then sprinting back to the three-point-line while player 5 flashes to the half court line to receive the long pass from 1.

Player 4 begins his cut to the top of the key looking for a pass the moment 5 gets the ball.

Player 5 catches the ball and looks to pass either to 2 or 3 or 4 for a shot.

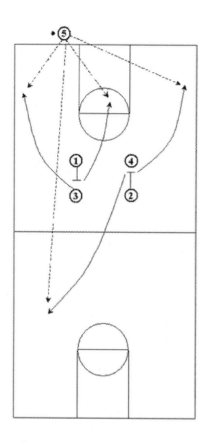

Late Game Situation
Inbound One

This press breaker works extremely well against teams that pressure the inbound pass. If your team is struggling to get the ball inbounds, try this play and I can almost guarantee you'll see a big difference and reduce turnovers

Player 1 back screens for 3 and rolls to baseline asking for ball and 3 cuts to the ball side wing.

At same time player 2 screens for 4 and pops out to the ball side corner looking for the pass from 5.

Player 4 comes off the screen by 2 running down the court looking for the long pass from 5.

Note: This is a good way to inbound the ball to any player and beat the press.

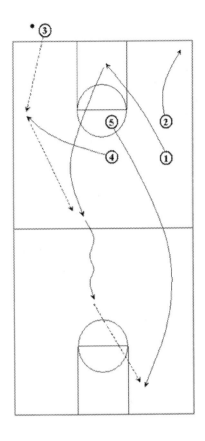

Late Game Situation
Inbound Two

Here is another good play to inbound the ball and beat the press in late
game situation.
Player 1 cuts into the lane to get the inbound ball from 3.
At same time player 2 breaks to right corner.
Player 4 pops out to the ball side wing to get the inbound pass from 3
and 5 sprints down the court.
Player 1 flashes to the mid-court to get the pass from 4.
Player 1 dribbles down the court and passes to 5 for a shot.

Full Court Shooting Drills

Use these drills during practice to prepare your team for the last second situations of the game.

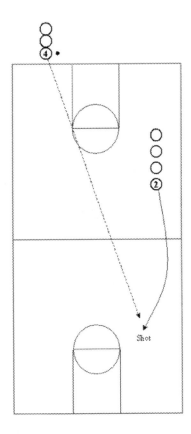

Catch and Shoot Drill

Player 4 the inbounder throws the ball to 2 who runs down the court to catch and shoot.

Note: All the players have to take a turn both throwing and catching the ball.

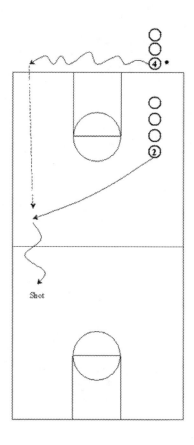

Baseline Run Drill

Player 4 the inbounder runs baseline and throws the ball to 2 near the half-court line
Player 2 catch the ball dribble twice and shoots.

Note: All the players have to take a turn both throwing and catching the ball.

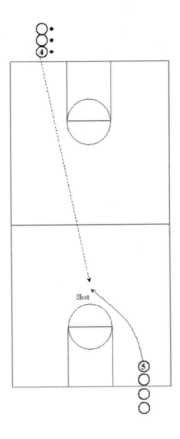

Big Man Flash Drill

Player 4 the inbounder throws a long pass to 5 who flashes to the top of the key to catch and shoot.

Note: Big players only have to take a turn both throwing and catching the ball.

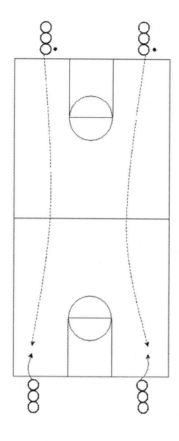

Long Pass Back and Forth Drill

Players will practice the long pass back and forth.

Note: All the players have to take a turn both throwing and catching the ball.

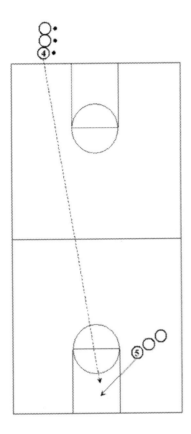

Tip-In Drill

The inbounder throws a long pass close to the rim.
Player 5 explodes to the hoop to catch the ball up in the air and tip in.

Note: Big players only have to take a turn both throwing and catching
the ball. Practice this drill of both sides of the basket.

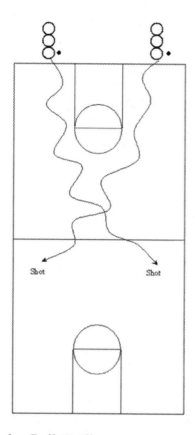

Push the Ball Drill

Players have 4 seconds to push the ball very quickly down the court for a shot after the half court line.

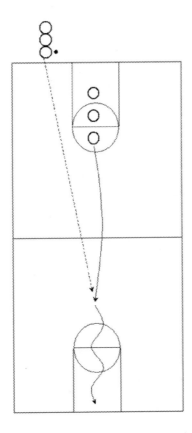

Catch Lay-Up Drill

Players sprint down the court to catch the ball near the three point line
for lay-up without dribble.

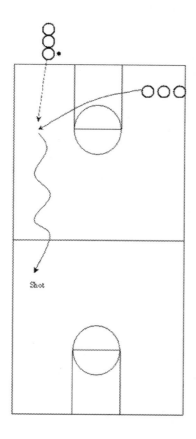

Catch and Dribble Shooting Drill

Players flash to the ball side to receive the pass then quickly push the ball after the half-court line for a shot.